Dilemmas and Decision Making in Social Work

Other books you may be interested in:

Children Forsaken: Child Abuse from Ancient to Modern Times
Steven Walker   ISBN 9781913453817

Fostering for Adoption: Our Story and the Stories of Others
Alice Hill   ISBN 9781914171239

Living a Good Life with Dementia: A Practitioner's Guide
Liz Leach and Jayna Patel   ISBN 9781914171567

Social Work and Covid-19: Lessons for Education and Practice
Edited by Denise Turner   ISBN 9781913453619

*The Anti-racist Social Worker: Stories of Activism by Social Care
and Allied Health Professionals*
Edited by Tanya Moore and Glory Simango   ISBN 9781914171413

Our titles are available in a range of electronic formats. To order, or for details of our bulk discounts, please go to our website www.criticalpublishing.com or contact our distributor, Ingram Publisher Services (IPS UK), 10 Thornbury Road, Plymouth PL6 7PP, telephone 01752 202301 or email IPSUK. orders@ingramcontent.com

Dilemmas and Decision Making in Social Work

Abbi Jackson

First published in 2021 by Critical Publishing Ltd

British Library Cataloguing in Publication Data
A CIP record for this book is available from the British Library

ISBN: 9781914171208

This book is also available in the following e-book formats:
EPUB ISBN: 9781914171215
Adobe e-book: 9781914171222

Cover design by Out of House Ltd
Text design by Out of House Ltd
Project management by Newgen Publishing UK
Printed and bound in Great Britain by 4edge, Essex

Critical Publishing
3 Connaught Road
St Albans
AL3 5RX

www.criticalpublishing.com

PAPER FROM
RESPONSIBLE
SOURCES

Contents

Acknowledgements

With gratitude to social work friends, practice education colleagues and students past, present and future. Thank you for the learning.

Meet the author

Abbi Jackson has worked in Children's Services for around 25 years. She has been a foster carer and has worked in secure care and children's residential care. She has spent time as a social worker in a statutory childcare team, as an independent Form F assessor and as a supervising social worker. She has led large-scale practice audits in Children's Services and more recently in adult protection. Currently, she is a senior planning officer for adult social work and integrated services in a local authority area and is an independent panel member for a private fostering company.

Abbi is also an active practice educator and lectures in critical social work practice. She has an interest in early intervention with young people who experience emerging mental health concerns. Never a dull moment, she is currently undertaking a piece of action research with young people receiving alternative therapies. She is a beekeeper in her spare time.

Author's note

Please note that the material in this book has been developed from the thoughts of the author as an individual and is not endorsed by any employer, past or present. The examples are fictitious.

Introduction

Welcome! It's great to have you here. This book has been written to help guide you in applying theory to social work practice. The stories in the chapters ahead are of fictitious characters told from the viewpoint of the social worker who is trying to help them. The interventions are not perfect examples (if these even exist). However, they give an indication of some of the social workers' thinking during practice; how they consider ethical dilemmas, how they weigh up options and how they work with other professionals. The stories provide insight into different areas of social work practice, while always regarding the person receiving support as the expert in their own life.

However, no one-dimensional account can offer a full understanding of the experience of the social worker in these stories. I want you to read attempting to imagine how this might look, sound and smell in practice. I want you to stop and reflect on what you would be feeling if you were in the role of the social worker: the frustrations and anxieties, butterflies in the stomach when you sense tension mounting, a tight throat when you want to say something but hold back or the sense of relief when you are able to retreat to your car after an intimidating encounter. Think alongside the storyteller about practice options in the moment, wonder if you are doing the right thing. This book is about reflecting *in* action (while it is happening) as well as *on* action (after the event). Consider the satisfaction that you have influenced improvements to someone's well-being and opportunities or where the intervention could have been different.

You can use the book in any way that fits for you. The side boxes noting approaches and theory to inform or intervene are intended as pointers towards good places to start reading. They are *not* the definitive answer. Please critique the theories noted and consider how they apply in each case. Discuss your thoughts with others and reflect upon where you would apply different theories. Use the case studies to explore the wider issues and themes raised, and how they apply to your practice.

Think about the balance in social work between justice, care and control, and the stages of change that apply in the stories. Especially consider the value-based practice and micro-skills you would use to attempt to retain a positive working relationship with each individual person. Debate what is a skill, what are values and what is an approach.

Perhaps you could pair up with someone and have a go at trying to defend the decision making in the stories or present to your practice educator or peers what you would do differently. Explaining your decision-making rationale competently and clearly in day-to-day practice helps you empower the people you serve. Accountability is being able to justify to multiple audiences exactly why you made specific decisions. Think about what a professional from another discipline would make of your rationale and if they might hold a different point of view. Consider how you would justify your decision making to the people and families in the stories if they held a more hostile position or distorted perspective. Debate congruence where you (the worker) and the service user align with understanding and expectation.

Perhaps you could discuss in supervision the dilemmas raised and critique the evidence base available alongside your own practice contexts. Consider what you do not yet know in these cases. Use this as a foundation to developing your own reflexive practice.

Practice educators could extend these uses of the material in the chapters according to their students' learning needs. Perhaps the background of the cases could be used in an action learning set in group supervision. Or further context could be added to the cases for discussion – for example, how do we approach the shadowy figure of Harry, who may, or may not, pose a risk to baby Sophie in Case Study 5? Perhaps supervision could look at what the person we serve would say if they were in the room.

You may want to consider the cases using the following diagram.

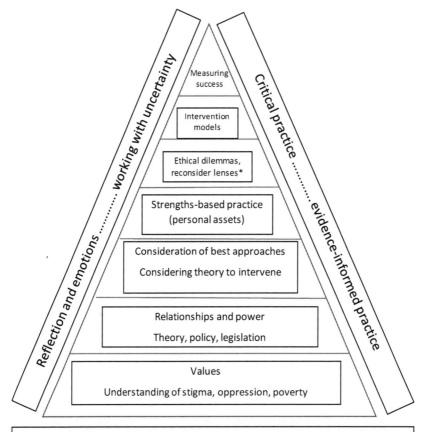

working with uncertainty

Critical practice

Reflection and emotions

evidence-informed practice

Measuring success

Intervention models

Ethical dilemmas, reconsider lenses*

Strengths-based practice (personal assets)

Consideration of best approaches

Considering theory to intervene

Relationships and power

Theory, policy, legislation

Values

Understanding of stigma, oppression, poverty

Building blocks of social work practice

*Looking through alternative lenses of:

human development, age, gender, ethnicity, culture, religion, disability, trauma, domestic abuse, relationships, sexual orientation, learning needs, literacy ability, neurodiversity, poverty, stigma, HIV status, mental or physical health needs, family systems, carer status and identity, personality, relationship with authority, capacity, criminal history, unmet need/neglect, recovery, rehabilitation, relationships with substances, addictions, loss and grief, housing and homelessness status, world view, other professionals' views.

What lenses would you add?

Case Study 1: Kim

Kim (aged 15) lived with her mum and her mum's half-sister (Maxine and Jill) and came to the attention of services when Jill was admitted to hospital after an intravenous heroin overdose. I was allocated the case soon after. The family were all hostile to each other and to social workers. Maxine had some learning difficulties but no diagnosis. Kim had had social work involvement before she started school and had spent time in foster care. However, she was very good at covering for Maxine and Jill as it turned out Jill had used heroin for a number of years. We soon realised that although Kim was acceptably turned out and able to sustain school life, the house was barely habitable. For example, the only reason they hadn't sold the cooker was because it didn't work properly. They had no carpets downstairs, no fridge or washing machine. Maxine was going up and down to her parents' house to wash clothes and they rarely had fresh food. They had often been arguing about money and this had previously involved low-level violence between all three family members. At the point I became involved Jill had decided to accept a methadone prescription. Their volatility towards each other and hostility towards services was then at its peak and Jill had been breaking her bail conditions (connected with supplying drugs in a children's play park). I found this out after the conditions had been lifted. Kim had known this and had been taunting Jill that she would 'grass' that she had been walking through the play park when they had family rows. She, in turn, was controlling towards her.

The dilemma was around how Kim's needs, both safety and welfare, were being provided for. She needed her carers to change to provide adequate care for her and while Jill stabilised on her methadone prescriptions the risk was high in terms of her becoming aggressive and, in Kim's words, 'getting in my face'. I would easily have had grounds to pursue care for Kim elsewhere. My dilemma was that if that were to happen, her attachment to her mum was so strong and her survival instincts so well developed that there was a real risk she would abscond and make her way home. Her feisty and determined

Margin annotations:

THEORY: Arousal–relaxation cycle

THEORY: Collusion, learned behaviour

THEORY: Addiction

THEORY: Dependency, stigma, addiction, cycle of change

INTERVENTION: Crisis intervention

THEORY: Need and risk, child development

THEORY: Attachment, learned behaviour

INTERVENTION: Secure base model

personality was likely to mean that she would not stop until she had reached what she considered her 'safe base' with her mum. I realised that may start to bring different patterns of behaviour and much higher risks. Also, all three were fiercely adamant that Kim was staying in the family home.

THEORY: Shame, guilt, power, attachment

In the early days, I did several visits in a short space of time (with another worker) to get a better understanding of risk, especially in regard to sourcing, storage and consumption of heroin. We sorted out some basic things, like electricity a couple of times, and facilitated their access to a second-hand fridge. This gained their tentative trust. I used local processes to bring professionals together to form a protection plan. The headteacher opposed my proposal of Kim staying with her family based on her school attendance over the previous year. We agreed to monitor this. I figured that we could make progress with attendance more readily than we could manage risks brought by absconding. Kim was also 15 years old so the risks were less than they would be for a much younger child. As agreed with the professional group, I looked at options for other family members where Kim could stay. I quickly ruled them out and documented the rationale. This also appeared to gain some trust from Maxine who agreed with my assessment and said she could have told me the same.

VALUES: Non-judgemental

THEORY: Need

THEORY: Unconditional positive regard, object relations theory, trauma-informed

INTERVENTION: Balancing risk and need

The over-arching barrier in this case was that Jill liked to talk really fast, continuously, and bring every conversation around to herself and her own needs and preferences. I figured that I needed her on side and spent a couple of visits just getting to know her. However, I realised she could control conversations to distract workers, so at the point where the family were beginning to be more willing to let us in the house, I proposed to her that we would need equal time speaking if I were to help them. She did not really respond to this, but I reminded her a few times!

THEORY: Psychoanalytic – defence mechanisms

THEORY: Nurture, trauma-sensitive

VALUES: Tolerance, compassion, kindness

INTERVENTION: Narrative approach relationship-based practice

INTERVENTION: Use of power

It would have been easy to allow Jill to control the direction of the work by the blocks she attempted to achieve. She had quite a fixed mindset on a lot of subjects – it appeared to be how she experienced the world. On one visit

THEORY: Mindset

she was hostile, turning her back on me and staring out of the window smoking, but not speaking. She was being intentionally intimidating. I had thought of ignoring her and carrying on the conversation with Maxine, even though I felt quite uneasy. However, I was mindful that this family continued round and round the drama triangle, and the only way I figured I could manage this was not to play into her casting of me as 'victim'. She had previously accused me of not being straight with her. So, this time I decided to be neutral and said quite directly and pointedly '*Jill, are you speaking today or not? I don't mind either way.*' This was not the way I would speak with most people and it could have provoked her to start shouting. I felt I could manage this risk though. However, without turning round, she instructed Maxine to speak to me about a couple of things.

THEORY: Coercive control

THEORY: Drama triangle

Interestingly, my approach on this visit, although I was unaware of it at the time, served to strengthen my relationship with all three of the family in different ways. Kim said eventually, much later, '*I'm only letting you see my bedroom because you were not scared of Auntie Jill that time.*' Maxine had then smiled knowingly. I could not claim that this was intentional relationship-based practice, but I had followed up my new stance with Jill, on the next visit, telling her that she could expect me to 'tell it like it is' and that however 'things go', I would be honest and open, including saying things she might not like to hear but she would have plenty of chances to talk things through and could disagree whenever she chose to. I said, '*I am listening – I might not always agree but I'm up for discussion.*' I had figured that Jill had not gone through her stages of development very successfully and she presented like an adolescent with some identity issues. From then on, I wrapped up each conversation with her clearly as 'the things we agree on', and 'the things we don't yet agree on'. This seemed to provide her with a sense of autonomy, and I thought that it responded on some level with respect to the trauma she may have experienced.

INTERVENTION: Relationship-based practice

VALUES: Transparency, respect, trauma-informed

INTERVENTION: Unconditional positive regard

THEORY: Human development

THEORY: Trauma, unmet need

I could see that Jill liked to dwell on the negative. She liked to have authority in the family, but Maxine did not seem to be disempowered by this and could equally speak her mind.

THEORY: Personality, emotional and psychological development

THEORY: Family systems, ecological model (exosystem), transactional analysis

INTERVENTION: Crisis intervention

THEORY: Ecosystems, family dynamics

INTERVENTION: Crisis

THEORY: Dependency, resilience, self-efficacy, coping

VALUES: Person centred

THEORY: Stigma, identity, child development

VALUES: Empowerment, respect, collaboration

THEORY: Need, transitions

INTERVENTION: Solution focused

INTERVENTION: Anti-oppressive practice, strengths-based practice

THEORY: Family systems and family hierarchies

INTERVENTION: Relationship

I was present at one point when all three of the family members were shouting and swearing at each other and I was placed in the role of a parent mediating. At the time I was aware again about the drama triangle, and my role in it. I had played 'rescuer', which was necessary to de-escalate things. I had to consider my part in this family system and how I was responding to their crisis. Once they had seen I was not going to shy away from their volatility they became less hostile but began to overshare their day-to-day struggles. I was careful to emphasise where the responsibility lay for resolution of these to reduce the possibility of dependency.

Maxine wanted Jill involved in all our discussions but I had to work really hard to get Jill to talk about Kim's needs; all she could focus on in this respect was that she did not want her to end up in secure care like Maxine had been as a teenager. We had found some ground to agree on and then had to find a way to work to meet her needs – all 'building blocks'.

I considered my timing, and when Jill was beginning to stabilise on methadone, and some of the basic needs had moved on, I did a little piece of work with them where they each wrote down (in secret) three positive qualities about the other two. I didn't know if they would participate but they surprised me. I then read these qualities out and the subject person was invited to accept or reject the comment. (They accepted all comments.) I then asked them to write down two reasons why this family was 'worth saving'. Kim wrote *'Auntie Jill is the only one who can get rid of spiders.'* This opened up a more productive discussion and I think set the tone for further engagement and collaboration as Jill struggled to stabilise on methadone and shift the family dynamics from Kim self-parenting to Maxine being able to focus on Kim rather than being wrapped up in her half-sister's needs.

Reflections

I think I did the right thing by not suggesting that Jill leave the family home to stabilise on methadone. Mayber her hostility and distraction techniques were based on this fear. She had lived there since Kim was two or three and they were a tight-knit unit. Even though she was volatile, Jill played a key role for Kim by helping her with homework and guiding her sensibly when she needed to sort out disputes with friends. This was more than what Maxine could have done. I get the sense that Jill has claimed Kim fully and wondered if that was because she may not have considered it possible to have a child of her own. However, this was not the time to explore this.

I saw the full risk where drugs were prioritised over Kim's basic needs; there was family tension and hostility, violence and, in my mind, a big risk of absconding if we removed her from Maxine. Kim refused to come downstairs, and Maxine and Jill did not permit me upstairs. This made me anxious. However, I believed that it gave me scope to keep coming back – probably more regularly than I would have with other early cases but that was to do with risk level. And it turned out right to work with them all together. I am glad I gave Jill my time at the start, so she felt validated. Although I was sure of my risk assessment and management plan, I was also conscious that my decision making had to stand up to evidence-based scrutiny and the risks were high. (I also figured that it would be hard to find a foster carer that Kim would respond to, having made decisions for herself for a long time. Foster care would have been far removed from her lifestyle and expectations of being cared for.) If Kim was younger the risks would have been different, and if she wasn't so resilient, a different risk management plan would have probably been better.

I had to set clear boundaries about what was appropriate for Jill and Maxine to talk about with Kim present and that when she was around, the conversation had to be about her needs and development. This, predictably, was hard for Jill and I had to insist a couple of times that we take a break and move to the kitchen to chat. This might not have worked well with other families. I believe that the three-way talks showed

VALUES: Ethical practice, integrity

THEORY: Object relations, family systems

INTERVENTION: Relationship based

INTERVENTION: Anti-oppressive practice, relationship-based practice

THEORY: Power

THEORY: Assumptive world, operant conditioning, trauma-sensitive, loss and change

THEORY: Resilience

VALUES: Inclusion

THEORY: Use of power and authority

THEORY: Communication

VALUES: Explicit honesty, integrity, sensitivity

THEORY: Self-regulation, co-regulation

VALUES: Tolerance, patience, reliability, respect

them I was not put off by their shouting at each other and when they asked that I 'be direct' with them I changed my approach to being more succinct in choice of language and more open about what I was thinking and the risks as I saw them emerging in the moment. This paid dividends I think, as it reassured them there was no hidden agenda. I was probably more forthright with this family than I am normally with others. All the time I was having to manage my anxiety and that of my co-worker (not the same person each time) as the family's presentation was quick to show very vocal annoyance and they were very challenging to manage with everyone speaking at once. I think it worked OK in the main because I firmly took the role of a nurturing but authoritative parent, working with the child parts of Jill.

Reflective questions

• Have I got the balance right between care and control?

• Have I indulged the family because I am struggling to manage my own anxiety in the light of their volatility?

• Am I able to truly lay out my decision making for the family to understand?

• Have I got a secondary plan if the first plan becomes too risky? What does that look like from the child's perspective?

• Could I have focused more on assets of the family and would this have improved their parenting quicker?

• At what point am I allowing a service user to control the relationship between us?

Further reading

Payne, M (2006) Narrative Therapy, 2nd ed. London: Sage.

Rivett, M and Buchmuller, J (2017) Family Therapy Skills and Techniques in Action. London: Routledge.

Sawyer, E and Burton, S (2016) A Practical Guide to Early Intervention and Family Support: Assessing Needs and Building Resilience in Families Affected by Parental Mental Health and Substance Misuse. London: Jessica Kingsley.

Tait, A and Wosu, H (2016) Direct Work with Family Groups: Simple, Fun Ideas to Aid Engagement and Assessment and Enable Positive Change. London: Jessica Kingsley.

Case Study 2: Josie

Josie was a lady in her early 40s. She had come from 500 miles away to live with Bill, whom she had met online three years ago. During their relationship, Josie had enjoyed cooking and home decorating but had no social connections outside the house. Josie was asthmatic and significantly overweight. Her weight had increased further since she had lived with Bill. Gradually she stopped doing home decorating as she could not bend very well, and the house became quite chaotic and unkempt. Josie began ordering everything online as it was easier for her – she was embarrassed about her weight and would not answer the door if she did not know people were coming as she could not get there quickly enough, but also because she did not want to see anyone.

THEORY: Assumptive world, transitions, loss and change, identity

THEORY: Isolation/Inclusion

THEORY: Motivation, cognition, obesogenic values, decision-making theory, emotions, self-efficacy

THEORY: Rational choice

THEORY: Shame

Josie's self-care began to deteriorate. Over time Bill had become her carer (albeit he did not prioritise the house-work either). Josie is not likely to have been easy to care for, but Bill did not ask for help and appeared to have been quite self-sufficient in many ways. For instance, when Josie had toothache and the dentist would not make a house visit, Bill had removed Josie's tooth with pliers himself. As Josie had increased in weight, he had started to help her to wash and change her clothes, which had become difficult due to her size and his physical capacity.

THEORY: Need

THEORY: Relationship dynamics, learned behaviours, dependency, motivation, need

THEORY: World view

THEORY: Behavioural reasoning, problem solving

THEORY: Need

Tragically, last week, Bill collapsed and died across the street from the house. Josie had seen him collapse from the window. To her credit she did attempt to go out of the house, which was the first time she had done in months. As Josie was very overweight, she stumbled in her haste and fell down the house steps. She got herself wedged between the edge of the concrete steps and the old car with no wheels that Bill had put up on blocks in the driveway. Josie lay there – stuck fast.

THEORY: Bereavement

THEORY: Motivation

THEORY: Helplessness, disempowerment

Neighbours had come to assist Josie, who was highly distressed. Josie did not know at this point that Bill had passed away, but neighbours stayed with her while a second ambulance crew tried to free her. Their attempts were not successful, and the fire brigade had to be called

THEORY: Ecosystems

INTERVENTION: Crisis

THEORY: Bereavement, complex grief

INTERVENTION: Trauma sensitive

THEORY: Need

INTERVENTION: Crisis intervention

THEORY: Locus of control, attribution

INTERVENTION: Crisis intervention

THEORY/INTERVENTION: Crisis

VALUES: Non-judgemental

to winch the car forward. Josie was taken to hospital for a check-up. It was there that she was informed that Bill had passed away.

The hospital alerted social services to Josie's poor presentation and personal hygiene. She was very upset that Bill had passed away. She was discharged from hospital in a couple of days however, when she was physically able to move around.

I had visited Josie to make an initial assessment. After I had gained the information about the situation, I offered her some care at home services. Josie appeared not to have an opinion either way. I think she was still in shock and was clearly blaming herself that she could not make it across the street to save Bill. On today's visit, I had planned to try again to pursue the possibility of having someone to come in and clean the house, and to pursue the occupational therapy service with them who could assess Josie's needs with the view to providing mobility aids and equipment to help her use the toilet.

I could hear shouting from within the house when I arrived. The house was as cluttered, dirty and unkempt as it had been at the start of the week. The place smelt badly and there were what looked like possibly bits of human faeces on the floor. I did not sit down, as there was nowhere to sit, but also, I was not sure of the cleanliness of the furniture or if I would need to leave quickly. I asked how she was, and Josie said that she could not move around in the house because her neighbours think she is cooking Spanish food for the cat. She advised that she wanted to do a crossword, but she could not because they were shouting at her; but I didn't hear anything except the low background television noise. I wondered at that point if the shouting I had heard on arrival had been Josie herself. I became more concerned for Josie's mental health and well-being and her capacity for decision making. I decided that she would need further assessment in that respect.

I did wonder about what assessment had been made in hospital prior to discharge about Josie's ability to care for herself, but then her well-being may have deteriorated in the

18 hours or so she had been at home. Additionally, she may not have acknowledged to the hospital staff that Bill had taken such a significant caring role for her. I knew I must be completely open with my intentions to respect Josie's dignity and human rights. Before I approached discussion about an assessment, I wanted to gain a bit of rapport. I asked Josie how well she knew the neighbours. She said they were okay, but now that *'this had all happened'* she did not want to see them ever again. I validated this by saying that this must feel difficult for her. She seemed humiliated Josie began making a wheezing sound which sounded quite alarming to me. I asked if she needed anything and she pointed to an inhaler on the side table.

When she had used this, Josie's breath returned to normal and she said that the neighbours did not want her to move. She then reacted as if she appeared to be hearing noises coming through the wall. I was certain that there was no sound. She then kicked the side of the vacant armchair and made a clatter as the items all fell off it. She chuckled but this behaviour was not in keeping with the situation.

I could not decide if this was an intentional distraction on Josie's part or if she was genuinely experiencing derealisation. I needed more information to make an initial assessment in the moment if she could be safely left to care for herself.

I asked when Josie had last seen a doctor for her breathing and she said she was not sure but a few months ago probably. She insisted that she was fine and that she would call the doctor if needed. I asked if any other 'health people' had visited recently as I wanted to try and get a gauge on when the situation had begun to deteriorate. Josie said that they did not need anyone else and told me not to worry. She was referring to Bill as if he were still alive, which of course is not uncommon for recently bereaved people. I have done it myself. It made me wonder about her orientation to the present though, given her behaviour today. I told her that I was a bit worried since she had had such a dreadful shock and that can make people short of breath sometimes. I did not want to focus directly on her obesity issues in this visit as there were more pressing concerns today. She said that she had had asthma for years and that they had given her two more inhalers when she came home from hospital. This seemed reasonable. I knew that Josie had bruising from the incident but no broken bones or other injuries. I acknowledged gently to her that it might take a bit of time for her to feel better, as she must be feeling sore, and to come to terms with what has just happened. I said that it was my job to see if there was anything she needed that would make things easier just now.

INTERVENTION: Trauma sensitive

I turned to the matter of Josie's mobility. I referred to our previous conversation and that we have people who could help with maybe a piece of equipment that Josie could lean on to get about. Josie seemed keen and I said I could bring a colleague next time who knows more about what was available. I said *'We have lots of specialists in our team. They are all really helpful.'* Josie appeared willing to have other people in her house now which seemed to be significantly different from the limited information I had about her. I believed that I needed to be very sensitive to her view of herself if she was to accept my help.

THEORY: Need

INTERVENTION: Task-centred practice

APPROACH: Nurturing

THEORY: Transitions

INTERVENTION: Emotional intelligence, relationship-based practice

I suggested we have a cup of tea. I wanted to see how she moved about the house, and also if she could co-ordinate the sequence for herself which would let me assess if she was safe before I left. She was amenable to this and with great effort and some groaning, made her way, through to the kitchen. I was quite taken aback to see mountains of diet supplements, meal replacement slimming drinks and other weight loss products on the worktop. This could have filled a supermarket shelf. This was not what I expected.

THEORY: Cognitive dissonance, planned behaviour

THEORY: Identity, labelling, stereotyping, complexity

Josie did manage to make tea and whilst she was occupied, I asked her what kind of person Bill was. She was happy to chat about him. I avoided talking about the funeral as I was aware that the cause of death had not been confirmed at this point. As she was about to pour the tea, I said, *'Actually Josie, I have changed my mind. I probably shouldn't have a cup of tea just now as I forgot – I have to drive for an hour when I leave here and will just need the*

APPROACH: Narrative

toilet the whole way. You have one though.' I hoped that this—— VALUES: Sensitivity was plausible. We chatted a bit and I was reasonably satisfied Josie could be left on her own. Before I left, I made sure she had the office phone number that I had given her yesterday. She placed her hand over mine and told me with a tear in her eye that I was a *'lovely girl'*.

Reflections

I had not got very far with dealing with the state of the house which I had intended to address on this visit. I was foolish if I had even thought this would be a quick fix. However, I responded to what was happening in the moment and made some progress at least.

VALUES: Person-centred, ethical practice

I could have been a lot clearer with explaining the extent of my power and will redress this on the next visit. I thought that today's visit could have gone either way – Josie could have become really anxious and presented as angry or irritated with me and if I didn't establish a relationship she may have become hostile and resistant for the rest of my involvement. I think I trod a fine line between getting Josie's agreement for assessments and antagonising her.

VALUES: Authenticity, honesty

VALUES: Trust

INTERVENTION: Emotional language, relationship-based practice

I will get the mobility aids sorted out first, then make further assessment. I resolved to support Josie as best I could with funeral arrangements and did not want to forget to call her tomorrow. I know I have got a pressing caseload, but I felt she was so vulnerable, and I was worried that she might deteriorate, so I must remember to call her. I also needed to discuss home care services with her as this is not a situation that can be left. I didn't know her well enough to make full assessment but today, because of the way she presented at the start of my visit, I was concerned. I need to write up my case notes promptly and make a referral to mental health services. If Josie deteriorates when the office is closed, I want the out of hours team to know what had happened today and how I drew the conclusion that she was safe to be left to care for herself. They need to know that I have made a referral to mental health services so that they don't duplicate work.

VALUES: Sensitivity

VALUES: Reliability, trust, empowerment

VALUES: Integrity, empowerment

INTERVENTION: Crisis

I wondered about Josie's background and what had brought her to this point. I had yet to understand her attachment presentation. I know that I am not qualified to assess and propose any attachment style categorically, but I was curious to understand the relationship dynamics between Josie and Bill. Why had Bill not asked

THEORY: Adult attachment

for help, and who had bought all of the dieting products in the kitchen? Regardless of this I know we could do some enabling work. I am going to put some thought into some unanswered questions to help me develop my thoughts around Josie's protection needs.

Reflective questions

- What ethical principles apply in this situation?

- What are my own frames of reference telling me about this situation?

- What are the possible risks not so far identified? What do we still need to know?

- How should we approach this if Josie does not see the need to make changes?

- What questions should I prepare to ask on the next visit?

- Who else should I be collaborating with and what are the barriers to this?

Further reading

Britten, S and Whitby, K (2018) *Self-Neglect: a Practical Approach to Risks and Strengths Assessment*. St Albans: Critical Publishing.

Brownell, K D and Walsh, B T (2018) *Eating Disorders and Obesity: A Comprehensive Handbook* (3rd ed). New York: Guilford Press.

Dominelli, L (2002) *Anti-Oppressive Social Work Theory and Practice*. Basingstoke: Palgrave Macmillan.

van der Kolk, B (2015) *The Body Keeps the Score: Mind, Brain and Body in the Transformation of Trauma*. London: Penguin.

Case Study 3: Leo

Leo – well where do we start? I have such a lot of time for Leo but he is *so* challenging. He had been adopted at aged two by parents who hired a succession of nannies and private one-to-one educators to care for him. This has not turned out well. They had taken him to specialist after specialist in the search (in my opinion) to 'medicalise' his needs. They did one session of family therapy and abandoned it as (I believe) it was too painful for his mother to admit her failings. Leo has a diagnosis of Asperger's syndrome and autism. He presents as emotionally younger than his age because of his diagnosis and lack of socialisation, and he is highly intelligent.

THEORY: Attachment

THEORY: Attachment

THEORY: Medical model vs social model

INTERVENTION: Family therapy

THEORY: Loss, attachment

THEORY: Empathy, executive functioning deficit, theory of mind (autism)

I had started working with Leo when he was seven and he is now ten. At the point he left the full-time care of his adoptive parents (around three years ago), he was very challenging. When things did not go his way, Leo would simply urinate wherever he chose, although he could use the toilet perfectly well. My non-medical opinion was that some of Leo's behaviour was likely to be connected with attachment and developmental trauma. The emergency foster carers could not tolerate his behaviour but the second carers, who he was currently with (until today), were brilliant.

THEORY: Human development (age/stage)

THEORY: Cognitive abilities

THEORY: Social learning theory

THEORY: Attachment, trauma, family systems

They had reinforced their ground floor with garage paint under the flooring, so the urine did not soak through and do damage. He had gradually begun only urinating in his bedroom, and then less and less frequently. He was making great progress.

I had a call this morning from Shirley (the female foster carer) to advise that her husband, Peter, had found weedkiller in Leo's room poured into old skincare cream and make-up pots that he must have been taking from the bin over time. When Peter had questioned Leo, he had said that he was going to kill all three of them with the weedkiller, on a date that he would not disclose, because he loved them so much and they could all go to heaven together and it

THEORY: Attachment, loss, bereavement

would be OK because his other two mums would not be there as nobody would let them in.

Shirley was distraught because the previous week the neighbour's cat had died from chemical poisoning and she now suspected Leo was responsible. She thought he must have taken weedkiller from the neighbour as they don't keep it themselves. She wanted Leo moved immediately as she did not believe she could keep anyone safe if that was Leo's intent and Peter had already phoned the police. Shirley had removed the weedkiller 'for safekeeping' and, because of the relationship I had with them, I trusted that they would not behave in ways that would increase any risk to Leo's safety.

THEORY: Crisis

INTERVENTION: Crisis intervention

THEORY: De-escalation, arousal–relaxation cycle

I texted my husband to cancel our plans for the evening. (Not great, but he knew who he was marrying. He is a reasonable sort!) I spoke with the police who insisted they would attend even though I said I would take another social worker. However, I asked if they would not wear hi-vis clothing, and if it could be just one officer, to try and minimise Leo's anxiety.

THEORY: Anti-oppressive practice, arousal–relaxation cycle

When we got there, Peter and Shirley were in the kitchen and the atmosphere was understandably very tense. They were perceiving the risk as actual. Leo was in his bedroom. Peter said he had checked the browsing history on the family computer and Leo had been looking up other ways to kill an adult or child. I asked what Leo had been doing since this discovery, so I could assess the current risk. He had been watching TV.

If I am honest, I was uncomfortable working with this police officer, Sam, as I thought he had been harsh with a teenager previously, so I had briefed him before we arrived about Leo's complex presentation. I asked that I be the one to tell him that he could not stay in his house.

THEORY: Opposite of unconditional positive regard

THEORY: Complexity, resilience

APPROACH: Nurturing, relational

I introduced Leo to Sam and asked him if he knew why we were here. He said that Shirley had taken his 'garden stuff'. We ascertained some clarity on this description. I asked him to help me understand how it came to be in his room.

I didn't ask 'Why did you have it?' as I thought that was too direct and confrontational. He told us sheepishly that he needed it so that he could make sure he and Peter and Shirley could always be a family. I said I didn't understand, and he said he was going to kill them all probably in the next couple of weeks so that they could all go to heaven, then nothing could change as Carol ('my maths tutor') says that heaven is the 'last stop'. He then said, *'Peter and Shirley are the best parents ever and I love them over and over and will never stop!'*

THEORY: Anti-oppressive practice

THEORY: Object relations, self-efficacy

I took a bit of time to talk about people having different versions of love, although Sam looked pained. I then spoke about safety and how people need to be alive to look after each other. I continually assessed levels of risk. I said that we needed to find Leo somewhere else to stay tonight so that he and Peter and Shirley could be safe. Sam agreed and Leo became agitated. In front of him, so that nothing was hidden, and so I could support him to manage with Sam there, I called the office and spoke to my manager. He knew her from meetings and tried to grab the phone a couple of times.

INTERVENTION: Opportunity led

INTERVENTION: Opportunity led

VALUES: Respect, dignity, honesty, integrity, anti-oppressive

I recounted the discussion that Leo, Sam and I had just had to my manager, using simple language that Leo could understand. He could use it as a recap and reinforcement of the conversation and my assessment of the risk involved.

VALUES: Respect, transparency, anti-oppressive

I had already asked colleagues to start phoning round for potential placements for Leo before I had left. I have a great team and we all step into help each other in an emergency. His needs are well known in the team. We agreed that my manager would ask a social work assistant to come and support me in the house and we would stay until we could find somewhere that could offer an emergency placement to Leo.

INTERVENTION: Solution focused

THEORY: Maslow's hierarchy of needs

I was conscious that Shirley and Peter were still in the kitchen probably on tenterhooks. I asked if Sam thought one of them could come through and *'we can pick up with next steps later.'* I did not think there was a role for Sam at that moment and so talked in a language that was calming for Leo but hopefully Sam could decipher as intended.

APPROACH: Nurturing

THEORY: Arousal–relaxation cycle

He seemed to have assessed the risk similarly. He brought Shirley through, made small talk and then left. Shirley to her credit presented unruffled and started to bring out Lego. We three sat there and I explained to Shirley, in front of Leo, what the conversation had just been. I felt confident doing this in this way, as Shirley is a very experienced carer who understands how to manage risk, and more importantly, is completely child-centred and knows Leo. I utilised her at this point as his secure base to help him self-regulate. I knew Leo had never presented as a risk to carers or workers before. The weedkiller (the actual risk) had been removed. If I had not had a good relationship with Leo or known the risk I was working with, I may have been glad of Sam staying.

VALUES: Transparency, honesty, integrity

INTERVENTION: Secure base model

We played a bit with Lego and answered Leo's repeated questions about where he would be going tonight, with patience. In about 20 minutes or so, when he was calm, I asked Shirley if Peter 'liked Lego and might like to play'. Shirley read this accurately and swapped over with Peter. I invited them to swap for two reasons. Firstly, because I was worried that Peter did not know what was happening and might be concerned – this break would give Shirley a chance to brief him in private, but more so, that I wanted Leo to understand that Peter was not angry and could still play with him as normal, although Leo knew things were changing and 'not normal'.

THEORY: Self-regulation

APPROACH: Nurturing

THEORY: Loss of the assumptive world, loss and change

Again, I was relying on the couple's 15-year experience of working with traumatised young people to calmly change places and they did so seamlessly. Leo said immediately to Peter, '*Am I not allowed to love you? I do love you. More and more every day.*' Peter said, '*I appreciate being loved. Love to me is when you learned to say thank you to me in French for helping you to learn to tie your shoelaces, or when you shouted, "he's the best Dad," to that lady in the shop when we found ice-poles.*'

APPROACH: Emotional intelligence

My colleague, Amanda, arrived and I casually excused myself in a way that Leo did not become agitated. Of course, I found out that we needed to wait a bit longer for other colleagues to arrange a placement for Leo and, in the interim, I made plans with Shirley that Peter would go in the car with me to drop Leo off and Amanda would stay with Shirley for a bit. This was so Shirley could receive some emotional support. I was again using the secure base the foster carers had established for Leo to transition him to his next placement and also trying to provide a secure base for the foster carers.

As no crime had been committed, I made arrangements with Shirley that they would see Leo again in a couple of days. Shirley, albeit shaken, was pragmatic and professional. I asked her advice about when to tell Leo this. She also began quietly packing some essential overnight things for him.

THEORY: Arousal–relaxation cycle

INTERVENTION: Solution focused

THEORY: Transition

VALUES: Respect, empowerment, compassion

APPROACH: Inviting narrative approach

THEORY: Attachment

APPROACH: Listening

VALUES: Respect, dignity

INTERVENTION: Solution focused

Reflections

I was wholly relieved that there was no other child in this placement. I was working with micro-dilemmas all the way along to de-escalate things. And I was so thankful for who I was working with. These carers knew how to keep the child's needs first, even when they were shocked and under pressure.

I realised later that I was a bit shocked as well because at one point a couple of years ago Leo had said that he had loved me! His concept of the meaning of love was very concerning coming out of the blue with a plan! Was I actually at risk? I will probably never know. To protect myself a little, I did smile for a moment about the line of reasoning Leo had given – what has heaven got to do with mathematics? It's not light though, of course (and no hard feelings towards 'Carol').

I did not know about the actual risk and how much weed-killer it would take to kill someone and if Leo had enough to do this. However, in my mind, the risk was very high as Leo was completely serious about his intent. He will need to be formally interviewed, including about the cat.

THEORY: Transition (planned/ unplanned)

I feel responsible that this has come to pass. I had matched Leo with these carers and was really pleased with my work. Senior management had commended my practice especially the way I had managed his parents' challenging behaviours, to minimise his distress in transition into this placement. These carers had offered everything Leo needed to flourish. He was doing so well, and I could see that they were becoming invested in him. My feelings of self-efficacy about good practice in finding and nurturing this placement had put these carers at risk. When I left Leo at his new placement, I felt a heavy weight that it could have been a tragedy.

I managed today with the carers' help. The thing that stings the most is that I know I won't be able to talk openly about how I feel with my line manager. She is not my type of person and any support offered will be tokenistic. Luckily, I have really supportive peers in the team though.

Reflective questions

- Where are the areas for improvement in the practice of all parties?

- Where can I learn more about working with this level of need?

- What would I have done differently if I did not have a positive relationship with the child?

- What would I have done if I did not know the carers or share their values and approach?

- How did this connect to my previous experiences and world view?

- How can we ensure our own emotional needs are met within our support network?

Further reading

Baylin, J and Hughes, D A (2016) *The Neurobiology of Attachment-Focused Therapy*. New York: W W Norton.

Drury, C and Hills, J (2015) *Healing the Hidden Hurts: Transforming Attachment and Trauma Theory into Effective Practice for Families, Children and Adults*. London: Jessica Kingsley.

Patterson J et al (2018) *Essential Skills in Family Therapy: From First Interview to Termination*. New York: Guilford Press.

Perry, B and Szalavitz, M (2017) *The Boy Who Was Raised as a Dog: and Other Stories from a Child Psychiatrist's Notebook*, 3rd ed. London: Basic Books.

Schofield, G and Beek, M (2014) *The Secure Base Model: Promoting Attachment and Resilience in Foster Care and Adoption*. London: BAAF.

Case Study 4: Rashid

It had been brought to our attention in Out of Hours social work that the police had evidence Rashid may be a risk to his own four children. His wife, Brittany, had called the police as she had seen a naked picture of him on a social media site. When she had confronted him, he had said a woman had stolen his picture from a dating app and uploaded it. He had signed up for a free month trial of the app for fun, with no intention of taking a subscription. However, the free trial was three years ago and there had been activity on the account during this time. Concerning comments on this history had led police to further enquiries which revealed Rashid was in possession of a quantity of pornographic images, including several pictures of children being abused.

Police had requested that a social worker attend the family home along with them, to advise that Rashid needed to stay somewhere else away from the children until more investigations were possible. Rashid also needed to be arrested.

We waited until there was a good chance that at least two of the children may be in bed and knocked on the door. I stood behind Martin, one of the police officers, to ensure that he could use his authority to enter the home. He said that we were there to speak about the complaint the couple had made about the publishing of an intimate photograph.

INTERVENTION: Trauma-sensitive

THEORY: De-escalation

Brittany let us in. We knew from social work records that Aisha, the oldest of their two daughters (aged eight), was receiving support in school for behavioural issues, and the school nurse had offered Brittany some advice about how to manage her enuresis (bedwetting). All the children were in their bedrooms when we arrived.

THEORY: Socialisation? Grandiosity schema? Power and control? Minimisation? Identity?

The police cautioned and arrested Rashid. He was quite calm and told Brittany there was nothing to worry about. Brittany was shocked and started pacing around holding her hands to her head. Rashid told her that it was probably because he was Asian, and they had to investigate all Asians like this. Martin told him he was being arrested

THEORY: Arousal–relaxation cycle

THEORY: Projection, distraction, diffusion of responsibility, victim theory

due to evidence they had already established and being Asian was not the cause of arrest. Rashid told Brittany that he would get a good solicitor and the matter would be finished in no time as the information the police had was obviously wrong.

THEORY: Cognition? Minimisation, entitlement/ grandiosity schema

The police and Rashid all left, and I was on my own to support Brittany. I repeated that I am a social worker, and said my job was to hear what people are thinking and help with next steps. She did not know what to say or do. She kept pacing around. Aisha had come to the top of the stairs and saw her father leaving with the police. She was wide-eyed, timidly hovering and her mum ushered her down. Aisha could see she was agitated.

THEORY: Shock, grief, stress, trauma

I introduced myself to Aisha as a social worker – someone who helps people if they need it. Aisha just stared. Brittany told her that Daddy would be fine, that he just needs to speak with the police for a little while and Aisha did not need to worry. Her body language said differently.

THEORY: Anti-oppressive

THEORY: Communication, congruence

I asked Aisha if she had been asleep when we had arrived. She said, 'No.' I asked her if she was playing a game. She said, 'I had Mortimer out.' Brittany added, 'Her hamster.' I said, 'Aww, I had a hamster when I was little. His name was Hamish. Does yours go in a ball around the floor?'

VALUES: Sensitivity

I was trying to find some common ground to build trust, but also find a way of getting Aisha back to her bedroom without worrying her as I wanted to discuss a safety plan with Brittany. I did not think it appropriate to start this with Aisha present.

THEORY: De-escalation

THEORY: Emotional intelligence

Aisha looked at me warily but said, 'Yes he goes in a ball.' I said, 'I built a little course for Hamish with paint tins, and he went round and round in his ball when I was little – I must have been older than you then though – maybe about 12.' Brittany appeared to be dissociating by this point and I said to her, 'Do you want to go put the kettle on, and maybe I could go and meet Mortimer then you and me could have a chat.' I turned to Aisha and smiled to help take the tension down. 'Would I be allowed to meet Mortimer?'

THEORY: Traumatic dissociation, vulnerability

INTERVENTION: Co-regulation

I felt that Brittany's response was appropriate given the news. I thought she might cry if I showed her empathy in that moment, so as soon as Aisha agreed, I led her out of the room. Aisha asked, *'Where have the police taken my dad?'* I said, *'They will have taken him to the police station.'* She asked, *'What has he done?'* I said, *'I don't know fully, but the police just need to ask him a few questions.'* She asked, *'Will they bring him back?'* I said, carefully, *'They will probably take a while speaking about things, so he won't be back before you go to bed.'* I thought I wouldn't lie to her, as that would not help her process anything, nor help her trust professionals. But equally I could not guarantee when she would next see him, so I needed to be succinct and just deal with the immediate future.

VALUES: Authenticity, honesty, integrity

THEORY: Self-regulation

THEORY: Intervention underpinned by child development theory, anti-oppressive practice

INTERVENTION: Life-space work

I played for a few minutes with Mortimer and settled her down. I then excused myself and went to Brittany. She was in a state of disbelief. She did not want to accept that the police had significant evidence. I had texted my manager to let her know we were OK, and we would just be having a cup of tea. I needed to get Brittany to agree how she would keep the children safe.

INTERVENTION: Co-regulation

THEORY: Trauma, grief

VALUES: Sensitivity

THEORY: Emotional intelligence

THEORY: Denial

INTERVENTION: Safe lone working practice

Brittany kept repeating, *'This is really not happening, this is really not happening.'* I acknowledged that this was a huge shock to her and said that I was there to support her. She asked if the police thought he has done anything to their children. I said we needed to just take one step at a time, and that I didn't know what they thought as I had the same information as she did (which wasn't strictly true) but the police just needed to interview Rashid.

INTERVENTION: Risk management

THEORY: Trauma, grief, cognitive dissonance

INTERVENTION: Crisis

I said clearly that Rashid could not have contact with the children for the rest of the weekend. I added, *'That's not to say different decisions won't be made on Monday, but for now the best plan would be for him to find somewhere else to stay as a precaution.'* I received a text back from my manager saying, 'safety plan?' I texted back, 'will let you know'. This allowed her to see that I was OK. I wasn't irritated with her pressuring me, but I did know that she would have wanted me to get the work done here as

INTERVENTION: Risk management

quickly as possible as she probably had other visits being held back waiting for me to pair up with a colleague.

Brittany said, *'They do think that he's abused them, don't they?'* I said, *'I really don't know what they think Brittany, but tonight Rashid might contact you after his interview, depending on how that goes. How are you going to handle it if he does?'* She stuttered, *'I don't know. I don't know what to believe. This is his home, and he has not been found guilty of anything. I think he should come home and then we can speak, and he will tell me if he has done anything. He couldn't have done anything – I would have known. He needs my support.'*

THEORY: Denial, assumptive world

I repeated gently that the police were asking for Rashid not to be in contact with the children. And it was likely that the children would need to be interviewed. Brittany burst into tears and said that lots of people go on stupid dating sites and say stupid things but that doesn't make them all child molesters.

THEORY: Stigma

I agreed with her but said that we needed to ensure the children were safe as a first precaution and that it was normal in this kind of situation for someone accused to be asked to have no contact with children. It would be the same for any family until a proper risk assessment could be carried out. I said the other option would be for Rashid to come home but the children to go somewhere else. I did not think that this was a fair solution albeit temporary; however, I was mindful of Brittany's rights as a parent. Brittany said angrily, *'You are not taking them!'* I said quietly that I did not mean that, more that she had options to decide – she could take them somewhere else herself for a couple of nights until we were clearer on the situation. I talked through the dilemmas around ensuring the children were protected if she wanted contact with Rashid, but that really the best solution for the children was to stay in their own home.

THEORY: Empowerment

THEORY: De-escalation

THEORY: Empowerment

THEORY: Nudge theory

INTERVENTION: Motivational interviewing approach

INTERVENTION: Risk management, solution focused

THEORY: Attachment

I let Brittany know that the police would also have told Rashid not to come back home just now. Brittany then proposed if Rashid wanted to come home, she would tell him he couldn't and she needed time to think. The position she was coming to was reassuring in terms of protecting the children.

I asked her not to allow the children to talk with Rashid either for the time being and checked out that Aisha did not have a mobile phone of her own and was not on social media. I established that Rashid had no other means of contacting the children without Brittany knowing. I also asked Brittany not to speak with the children about anything to do with these issues. We then agreed what she would say to them about why Daddy is not here.

INTERVENTION: Risk management

INTERVENTION: Co-production

I found out what the family plans were for the following day (Sunday) and helped Brittany decide to do something different with the children in case Rashid decided to go where they had planned to be. Brittany agreed that she would keep her doors locked and that if Rashid did come to the house, she would distract the children and call the police. Rashid had left without his house keys.

I gave Brittany the Out of Hours number and called my manager and made plans with her and Brittany for the oncoming team tomorrow to make contact with Brittany to give her support and further guidance. I saw each of the children, who were all sleeping, and then left.

THEORY: Empowerment

INTERVENTION: Task-centred practice

Reflections

This situation was fairly straightforward for me. Although it was horrible, there was only one solution and that was for Brittany to agree how she was going to keep the children safe. If she had insisted that Rashid came home with the children still there, we would have had a bigger issue. Although I have done this type of work lots of times, I still get a bit quivery inside when I am trying to frame the options as such to the protective parent, when I really only want one outcome. I know I need to repeat myself so people can take it in, and do it in a way that is nurturing as well as with authority. One of my students once called working with involuntary clients *'insisting but in a kind way'*, which I think has some truth in it.

I know that I did not emotionally engage on a personal level with the presenting issue today, I was just doing a routine, goal-oriented, piece of work. My focus was firmly on the safety of the children. I probably should have asked if any of the younger children had access to devices but as they were all under age six, I made assumptions they did not. I helped Brittany manage immediate emotion as I kept calm, but now I need to rely on my manager to liaise with police and I can park all this and focus on the next visit.

INTERVENTION: Risk management

THEORY: Communication, cognition and stress response

THEORY: Anti-oppressive practice and empowerment

THEORY: Emotional intelligence, trauma-sensitive

INTERVENTION: Risk management

THEORY: De-escalation, co-regulation

Reflective questions

• What assumptions are implicit in this account?

• What has influenced successful collaboration between professionals and with Brittany?

• What don't we know yet about this family that would be essential to know?

• What are the risks of being overly optimistic that the family will stick to the safety plan?

• How does the theory of shame apply to the presentation of the adults in this case?

• How do we protect ourselves as workers against emotional fatigue?

Further reading

Dunhill, A, Elliot, B and Shaw, A (2009) *Effective Communication with Children, Young People, Their Families and Carers*. Exeter: Learning Matters.

Fowler, J (2008) *A Practitioner's Tool for the Assessment of Adults Who Sexually Abuse Children*. London: Jessica Kingsley.

Munro, E (2019) *Effective Child Protection*. London: Sage.

Nicholas, J (2015) *The Practical Guide to Child Protection: Challenges, Pitfalls and Practical Solutions*. London: Jessica Kingsley.

Case Study 5: Sophie

Sophie is seven months old. She is an alert smiley baby, albeit there are some concerns about her weight gain. Julie, Sophie's mother, is challenged with significant behavioural issues. She has not been diagnosed with any mental health condition but continues to refer to herself as having mental health problems at times when (in my view) it suits her to do so.

THEORY: Child development

THEORY: Attribution

THEORY: Trauma?

Julie's own parents both had mental health diagnoses. Julie's father was diagnosed as having schizophrenia before Julie was born. It seemed that he had not managed his condition consistently and had often been in hospital over the years. Her mother had a long-term diagnosis of bipolar disorder. In Julie's early teens her parents had divorced and Julie's mother remarried. However, Julie's father continued living in the family house with Julie, her mum and stepfather. Subsequently, Julie's mum and stepfather had divorced, and her stepfather had begun a relationship with Julie's paternal half-sister, Tricia. This relationship too had ended, and Tricia is now living with Harry, who has previously served concurrent prison sentences for sexual abuse of two children over a prolonged period.

THEORY: Trauma, family systems, relationships

There had been no pre-birth risk assessment done for Sophie as no significant issues were presented during pregnancy. Julie had not disclosed who Sophie's father was and, at the time, Harry was unknown in connection with the family. Julie's mother had accompanied her to antenatal appointments and as they both presented articulately and dressed well, there were no outward signs of concerns that could have been picked up in the very short appointments the midwives have got to make assessments. Some of Julie's previous volatile behaviour had become known after the birth, however.

I had become Sophie's social worker when she was two months old following concerns raised by health staff over Julie's ability to meet her needs. After a conversation I had had with Julie yesterday about how she was going to keep Sophie safe from Harry, Julie had gone on to purposely leave the taps on in her house to flood it. This escalated and police had needed to detain Julie so they could make her and her house safe.

Sophie could not be cared for by Julie's parents due to their own difficulties, so Julie's other half-sister Lucy was caring for her. Sophie was there during the incident.

Today I met with Julie to discuss the position, along with my colleague Sandra from Health Services. Julie was tearful from the start. We listened to her account of yesterday's events. Julie was adamant that she did not need me to tell her how to keep her baby safe and if I was to 'keep on speaking to her like that' she would 'just kick off again'. I stated neutrally that my aim was to work with Julie to help her until Sophie did not need me anymore. I tried to get Julie to see this reasoning, but she was not ready to hear. She was holding me responsible for her actions and said she messed the place up to 'take me down a peg or two'.

Julie's view was that as Sophie had not been in her care when she had behaved in a way that required police attendance, then Sophie was safe. She said she had not been 'kept' by the police or the mental health service where she had been assessed yesterday so she was not a risk. I was not going to argue directly with this, so I focused on discussing the basic needs of a baby and how Julie was providing for Sophie. Julie had effectively made herself homeless by rendering her tenancy uninhabitable. In a way this was helpful, as it bought services some time for wider assessment and support, while Sophie's needs were met elsewhere.

I asked Julie where she was now living, and she was vague. The way she was talking made me think she had stayed with Tricia and Harry last night. I asked her if she had spoken with anyone from the Housing Department about her house. She had not, so we agreed that Julie would make the initial call and I could support her to meet with them if she needed to, in order to discuss where she would live while the repairs were carried out on their house.

THEORY: Learned behaviour? Cognition, human development stages, moral development

THEORY: Defence mechanisms, attribution, rationalisation, locus of control

THEORY: Use of power

THEORY: Child development, need

INTERVENTION: Task-focused

THEORY: Anti-oppressive practice, emotional intelligence

APPROACH: Relationship-based practice

INTERVENTION: Solution focused

To facilitate Sophie's attachment development with her mum and Julie's bonding with Sophie, I believed that we needed to set up some clear arrangements where Sophie could spend some supervised time with Julie. I proposed this to her, and Julie began raising her voice saying she did not need to be supervised with her own child. I thought about portraying the supervision as a more convenient way of Julie seeing Sophie as she did not have a place to go herself until her house was repaired. However, I figured that this would just be setting up unhelpful expectations later and I needed to be clear about my risk assessment.

THEORY: Attachment and bonding

THEORY: Anxiety, distress

THEORY: Stigma, shame

I was aware of the dilemma that I currently had no legal grounds for insisting upon supervision, yet I needed to ensure Sophie's safety. I suggested that Lucy could supervise so it was just an arrangement within the family. Julie said that her mum would not like that, and her mum would do the supervision. Then she immediately said again that she did not need supervision and she would be going to collect Sophie after she 'finished with us'. I outlined the legal position, the risks that I saw (not mentioning Harry for the moment) and the action I would need to take if Julie did go round and collect Sophie. I spoke in a firm but fair voice and was supported by Sandra who reiterated back to Julie some of her own words about wanting the best for Sophie.

THEORY: Basic needs

THEORY: Family dynamics

APPROACH: Balance between care and control

THEORY: Motivation

APPROACH: Strengths-based practice

Julie continued to oppose the risk assessment and we had to go through each point another couple of times, saying that we needed to ensure that people were safe around Sophie and she was not exposed to danger. I tried to frame this in terms of need rather than risk, so that I was not continually triggering Julie by shaming her. At the same time, I believed that I should be really clear about expectations. I figured if I gave Julie my time and patience now then I could develop a better relationship with her which would help me meet Sophie's needs. I validated Julie as a person and as a mother and acknowledged her feelings. I spoke mainly in a level tone when Julie was agitated. Sometimes I purposely met her pace and tempo, and then slowed my own to help her match me and enable her to take in what was being said.

INTERVENTION: Crisis

THEORY: Need

THEORY: Window of tolerance, shame

THEORY: Emotional intelligence

APPROACH: Relationship-based practice

APPROACH: Trauma-sensitive

THEORY: Self-regulation

INTERVENTION: De-escalation

THEORY: Communication, empowerment

Julie did not agree she was a risk to Sophie but did concede that when she had started damaging her home, she felt she could not stop. She did agree she needed her house repaired before she and Sophie could go back and live there, and she did agree that Sophie needed a calm home. She repeated that she wanted her mum to supervise the time she spent with Sophie until she could have her back. I pointed out that she had an uneasy relationship with her mum and if they were to start shouting that would not be a calm environment for Sophie. I put the question back to her: *'What would you do if you were me? What would you suggest (apart from Sophie returning to your care right away – which we are going to work on together, right)?'*

THEORY: Family systems, family dynamics

THEORY: Empowerment

INTERVENTION: Solution focused, transactional analysis (adult-to-adult interaction)

Julie said that she did not want her mum and her sister falling out as she had had enough of this and did not want Sophie in the middle of it. I praised her for thinking of Sophie's best interests. Sandra talked about what stress does to babies and Julie looked like she understood this.

APPROACH: Relationship-based practice

THEORY: Arousal–relaxation cycles, biology of stress

INTERVENTION: Advocacy

I asked her if it would be best if I had a chat with Julie's mum and sister themselves and see if we could ask them to supervise Julie with Sophie together, and manage to do this agreeably with each other, for the next couple of days while the house was repaired. I expected the repairs would take longer than this, but we had to start with some level of family agreement, given that there were no legal grounds established yet. I thought this visit would give me a chance to risk assess the relationship between them to decide firstly whether the proposed supervision arrangements were suitable, but secondly whether Lucy is able to care for Sophie adequately for a bit longer or if we need to seek alternative arrangements. From what I knew of the family, I considered that Julie's sister was a buffer between her and her mum.

THEORY: Need

Julie agreed but said she did not want to be there for this discussion. I negotiated with her that she would go and get some lunch and I would go and speak with her mum and sister early afternoon and get back to her to discuss. She agreed to phone her sister to ask how Sophie was doing. Sandra took the opportunity to ask at this point about

Sophie's feeding routine, and if Lucy knew about this. Her questions were framed in a non-judgemental way which I found really skilful.

APPROACH: Trauma-sensitive

Julie said that Sophie had not been with her aunt for such a long time before although she had babysat a few times. Sandra asked Julie to write down what Sophie was fed and gently helped Julie make some tweaks to the timings of feeds. I agreed to take this note round to speak with Lucy, given that Sophie had been in her care for nearly 24 hours now, and it would be important to be accurate with her routine. I said to Julie that I would 'report back' to her as soon as I had spoken with both her sister and her mum.

THEORY: Need

APPROACH: Relationship-based practice, anti-oppressive practice

Reflections

THEORY: Anti-oppressive practice, validation

I had said 'report back' to give Julie her place as Sophie's mum, as she was working voluntarily with me. Would I have said 'report back' if there had been a legal order in place? I am not sure. Maybe. However, I felt like Julie was starting to agree with some of my risk assessment towards the end of our conversation. I wanted to try to keep her engaged with me and with the arrangements we had made. She had seemed to understand as well as agree to the plan (for now).

THEORY: Complexity, stress/ vulnerability

THEORY: Trauma, Bowen theory

THEORY: Cognition

I don't believe that we are going to be able to guarantee Sophie's safety in a few days if she returns to Julie's care. Julie has suffered relational trauma within her family dynamics and her thinking is quite distorted if she believes that flooding and damaging her house is retaliation towards a worker advising her on how to keep her child safe. She is also mistaken if she thinks her behaviour will deter workers – me especially. The neighbours had called the police due to the level of noise coming from the property yesterday and they thought there was a group of people inside. Julie's behaviour will be serving a function for her and she intended to attract attention. We need to see some stability before we can safely say that she can parent Sophie. Her volatility is worrying.

THEORY: Behavioural, functionalism

THEORY: Need, secure base

I want to know more about the family relationships. I will check out if Lucy has contact with Harry. Again, there is no legal order preventing Harry from contact with Sophie, so the safety plan relies solely upon family protecting her. I need to find out what both Julie's mum and sister know about Harry's background firstly.

THEORY: Use of power

I will definitely prepare paperwork in case we need to use legal means to protect Sophie. And I will do a written agreement of what we discussed with Julie today – the things that she needs to do to prepare for Sophie to come home.

Reflective questions

- What influenced successful collaboration with Julie here?

- If Julie had been more reluctant to agree to the safety plan, what other skills and strategies could I have used to encourage her to agree, other than using legal means?

- How do we start to understand Julie and how she functions at a deeper level?

- How does the outcome today fit with my ethical position?

- How would I need my supervisor to challenge me in this situation?

- How can I further use emotional intelligence in this case?

Further reading

Featherstone, B, White, S and Morris, K (2014) *Reimagining Child Protection: Towards Humane Social Work with Families*. Bristol: Policy Press.

Goleman, D (1996) *Emotional Intelligence: Why It Can Matter More Than IQ*. London: Bloomsbury.

Smith-Acuna, S (2010) *Systems Theory in Action – Application to Individual, Couple and Family Therapy*. Hoboken, NJ: Wiley.

Wolynn, M (2017) *It Didn't Start With You*. New York: Penguin Books.

Case Study 6: Elizabeth

Elizabeth is living in a privately rented house with her adult son, Victor. She agreed to receive a service to help her with her addiction to benzodiazepines and I had been asked to support her. Her addiction had begun as a prescription for diazepam and quickly escalated to Victor acquiring street drugs for her.

Elizabeth had previously held a job as a receptionist in a solicitor's office but had been asked to leave as at that time she had a problem with alcohol. She related this to her response to the death of her eldest son, Neil, in a car accident some ten years or so ago. Elizabeth was very shameful about her problems and had lost all her support network when she left work. She is especially concerned for Victor, as the death of his brother had triggered some mental health difficulties for him. Elizabeth blames herself for the accident as she and Neil had had a row prior to him driving the car. His partner had never permitted Elizabeth to see her granddaughter after this day and moved out of the area.

THEORY: Grief and loss

THEORY: Shame

THEORY: Grief and loss, change

THEORY: Grief and loss

THEORY: Need

THEORY: Guilt, attribution

THEORY: Grief and loss, change

Elizabeth's house is in very poor condition. Victor sleeps in one of the bedrooms but Elizabeth sleeps in the living room in her armchair as there is water coming through the ceiling in her bedroom. Victor lives in the house rent free and, because the house is relatively secluded, it is my suspicion that he finds it convenient that people can come and go unnoticed from the back door. I believe he may be selling drugs.

THEORY: Need

I have made some visits over the past few weeks to Elizabeth and spoken with her on the doorstep. She was ambivalent about receiving a service but kept asking me to come back. She let me inside the house last week and when I had a proper look I was quite taken aback at the level of disrepair. The house looked like someone had moved in but just not unpacked. There were no carpets down, albeit rolls of carpet were stacked up ready to lay. There were floorboards missing outside the bathroom which was very

THEORY: Need

THEORY: Risk

THEORY: Need

unsafe. This was compounded more so by the broken hall light which had wires hanging down. The place clearly had a mouse infestation and a significant damp problem. Elizabeth had had no hot water for over a year.

THEORY: Crisis? Learned behaviours? Resilience?

When I had seen the living conditions, I had asked Elizabeth if she and Victor could go and live with her sister temporarily while the work was carried out. However, her sister was prepared to offer a room to Elizabeth, but not to Victor. Elizabeth would not leave without Victor, as she was worried about him as he could not cook. She appeared not to be able to see him as an adult.

THEORY: Transactional analysis, human development/life course, transitions

Another reason for Elizabeth not wanting to live in the house anymore is because she has had a recent short-term relationship with the landlord, which has now ended. The landlord was refusing to repair the house stating that Elizabeth had caused the damage. While this could be said of some doors perhaps, it was not true of the house conditions in general. Elizabeth had been on the local housing list for about eight months. Her drug use had increased in this time.

THEORY: Need

THEORY: Stress – vulnerability, resilience

When I had come back from the visit last week, I had asked the Housing Department to inspect the current property, as I believed it was uninhabitable. Yesterday they had visited and advised me that the house did not fall below the minimum standard they would expect.

I had emailed at length and spoken with a colleague from the Housing Department as I still did not agree with their assessment. I believed that these housing issues were contributing to Elizabeth's reliance on benzos.

THEORY: Need

INTERVENTION: Advocacy

THEORY: Stress – vulnerability

My visit today was to speak with Elizabeth again about moving somewhere else while alternative accommodation could be found. She was in a low mood when I arrived. I explained what the Housing Department had said and my challenging this. She said that she had not told me the truth last time and she was behind on her rent. Her landlord would not do the repairs until the rent arrears had been cleared.

Elizabeth became tearful. She said that she could not keep up with everything as it was so expensive to live nowadays. She said she could not even afford the small payments for her phone and she hardly even uses it, so Victor now pays it. I asked if she would like to be referred for an income maximisation assessment. She said she was not entitled to anything else. Her deceased husband's pension should have covered the rent *'if the bills weren't so darned high'*. Elizabeth produced an electricity bill, which was, indeed, ridiculously high. I asked her if she had a tumble drier or any other bigger appliances. She didn't and she was only really living in the one room. I asked if there were any appliances in Victor's room – the only room I had not been in. Elizabeth said she didn't think so. I did not want to inspect this room as Victor was not present. I suggested that there may be a fault and she may need to contact the supplier.

THEORY: Poverty, need

THEORY: Dependency, enmeshment

THEORY: Stress – vulnerability

THEORY: Need

I asked Elizabeth if she had spoken with her sister again about the possibility of her and Victor moving in for a while. Elizabeth started crying again and said that she couldn't leave Victor on his own and Frances would not have him. She was so worried about him as he might try and kill himself again if she left. I asked if she had any indication Victor was suicidal at the moment, and she said she didn't know. I asked where he was and again, she said she didn't know. I tried to find out from her when the last time Victor had indicated that he might wish to end his life. Elizabeth started to tell me about Victor as a child, and I listened to her stories for a bit. She became deeply upset when she talked how things had gone wrong for him. I felt tears pricking my eyes as I felt her loss. I said I could see how sad this was making her. I wondered if I should have hugged her. I decided not to and struggled to regain my composure while still empathising. Elizabeth said that Victor was all she had left, *'plus, I need him to help me when I don't feel well and can't go out. He wouldn't be able to do that if I was with Frances.'* I suggested that she would have her sister for support, but she dismissed this. I suspected that the arrangement was convenient for Elizabeth to have a regular supply of benzos via Victor, but I did not say this.

VALUES: Inclusion

THEORY: Family systems

THEORY: Constructionism

INTERVENTION: Narrative

THEORY: Grief and loss

VALUES: Authenticity

THEORY: Learned helplessness, dependency

THEORY: Learned behaviours

THEORY: Shame, stigma

I also wondered if perhaps she was embarrassed and did not want her sister to know the extent of her problems.

INTERVENTION: Compassionate approach

I asked Elizabeth how she was managing her own health. She was vague and said she knew what she was doing. I tried to probe what she meant and established that she was worried about headaches and sickness. She said she would start the tablets again for depression and anxiety and

THEORY: Cycle of change, ambivalence

that she had a *'bunch somewhere from last year'*. I advised her that she needed to go back to the GP to talk about *all* her symptoms, as it would not be good to just start taking

THEORY: Medical model, social model

previously prescribed medication without advice. She chuckled dryly, saying that the stuff was useless anyway.

I asked her if she knew how the combination of her tablets and any illicit benzos would affect her. She flicked her hand to dismiss this. I thought about going through some

THEORY: Empowerment

possible side effects but decided to give her information to keep. I asked her if she had already taken the two together and she denied it. For safety, I asked her how many old tablets she had in her house. She seemed like she genuinely didn't know but eventually agreed that she would find them and take them back to the pharmacy. I wondered if she really did have any and was curious if Victor knew about these. I was querying my own understanding of his behaviours and was not fully sure of the risk Victor posed to his mum.

I reminded Elizabeth again that it would be best to visit the GP and explain any current symptoms. I pointed out that she had just said she wanted to look after Victor as she was worried about him and she would not be able to do that if she became very unwell. (I meant *'incapacitated due to substance misuse'* but chose my words carefully as

VALUES: Trust

it was early in our relationship.) She did see this reasoning and said, *'I hate being me.'*

I thought this was not getting us very far and we needed to focus on practical things. I was curious about the

THEORY: Co-dependency, power

co-dependencies between Elizabeth and Victor and wanted to explore their relationship. I saw a way of letting the conversation wind round to talking about Victor as, in my view, he was the elephant in the room. I asked, '*Have you had any further signs of mice, Elizabeth?*' She said that they were always there, and she puts cornflakes out in the kitchen for them to stop them coming near her in the night. I did not realise the situation was this bad, nor what Elizabeth was doing to exacerbate these issues. I advised her to put down traps instead and asked what Victor thought about the mice. She said, '*Oh he only eats and goes back to the garage or his room – you would have to ask him if he has seen mice.*'

THEORY: Cognitive distortion

I said, '*I didn't know you had a garage, Elizabeth.*' She said, '*You can't see it from the house. It's tucked behind my neighbours' wall. They probably can't see it either to be honest.*' Alarm bells started to ring for me, and I said casually, '*It must be dark for Victor down there in the winter, then.*' She gave me the answer I was hoping she might without me asking a direct question: '*Oh no, he has lights – always has done.*' Putting two and two together with Elizabeth's high electricity bills, I suspected why Victor might be spending time in the garage, and why he continued to want to live in a house in such poor shape and pay his mum's phone bill, but I said nothing. I needed to think about what to do with this information.

THEORY: Motivation, co-dependency

Instead, I said I could speak with someone from Environmental Health and get them to contact Elizabeth about the mice. We talked a bit about her anxieties and eventually she agreed to allow Environment Health in. I also discussed with her that we needed to let the Housing Department know how bad the infestation was. I was not convinced they had inspected properly. I asked Elizabeth to give them a ring, so we both had a task. I would also email them.

THEORY: Planned behaviour

INTERVENTION: Task-centred practice

INTERVENTION: Advocacy

Reflections

I was a bit tense after this home visit. I did not like it one bit that Victor had taken on the payments for his mum's phone. I was very suspicious that he had something to gain all round, not just free rent. It was all very enmeshed, and I really needed to dig deeper into these co-dependencies.

I also thought I needed to bring Victor into the conversations too as he was part of the support system around Elizabeth, as well as a probable risk factor. I really needed to get Victor on side so I could get into his room to get more information to support or disprove the fact that I thought that he was exploiting his mother.

I needed to pass the bit of intelligence I had onto the police but at the same time not put Elizabeth at risk. This was going to be tricky. Next steps – to hassle the Housing Department.

Reflective questions

• Which other professionals do I need to work with and what do I want them to do?

• How will knowledge inform my interventions?

• How can I begin to reconstruct the issues with Elizabeth?

• How can I work in partnership with Victor?

• How can I find Elizabeth's assets and work with these?

• How might success be measured in this case from the service user perspective?

Further reading

Allan, G (2014) *Working with Substance Users: A Guide to Effective Interventions*. London: Red Globe Press.

Crawford, K (2011) *Interprofessional Collaboration in Social Work*. London: Sage.

McTighe, J P (2018) *Narrative Theory in Clinical Social Work Practice*. Cham, Switzerland: Springer.

Thompson, N and Cox, G (2019) *Promoting Resilience: Responding to Adversity, Vulnerability and Loss*. New York: Routledge.

Case Study 7: Meikal

Meikal's teacher suspected something had changed when Meikal came in a few times in a school jumper that was too small for him. It was only when one of his classmates told her that Meikal was sleeping in his room with him every night that she was alerted to a bigger issue. It turned out that Meikal's mum's partner, Adam, had been released from prison four months previously and Meikal had been staying with a succession of friends ever since. Meikal was adamant he had opted to 'leave home' (at the age of 11) as he did not like Adam.

THEORY: Unmet need

THEORY: Rehabilitation, transitions

THEORY: Loss of assumptive world, ambiguous loss, transitions

THEORY: Lack of secure base, resilience, problem solving

I had been working with the family for three weeks and managed to find out that Meikal was frightened of Adam and had alleged Adam took cocaine. The fourth family who had recently taken Meikal into their home, and who were currently caring for him, were also frightened of Adam. They knew he had been in prison and assumed (incorrectly) this was for drug-related crime. He and his family also had a reputation in the community for intimidation. Adam and some of his family members were receiving mandatory services from community justice workers and the courts had specified that his two brothers should have no contact with their own children. However, Adam was not Meikal's father and had no other children. There was no legal order in place preventing his contact with anyone.

THEORY: Identity, stigma

INTERVENTION: Legal

We had made a couple of visits to discuss the situation with Meikal's mum, Bianka, and Adam had been present. He had been perfectly civil and denied taking cocaine. He said he liked Meikal and they got along fine. On both visits the dog was barking ferociously in the kitchen, clawing wildly at the door. Adam had apologised for this and advised pleasantly that he was training this dog (Rudi) as a guard dog for three hours every day and 'doing well with intruders'. Adam had said that he and Bianka had agreed, as parents, that Meikal could go for sleepovers with friends. Bianka had vaguely said that she would speak with Meikal about coming home. My dilemma was that although Bianka had parental rights, I was not convinced that it was safe for Meikal to come home, even though I had no evidence that Adam had harmed Meikal or was any risk to children.

THEORY: Power

THEORY: Power

THEORY: Planned behaviour

Meikal was a cheerful boy who did not present any behavioural concerns and was well-liked in his peer group. His current 'host' family were happy to have him stay short term, but his friend's mother was also caring for her own mother who had dementia and an aunt who was housebound, as well as Meikal's friend and his sibling. Her husband ran a business and perceived ultimately his livelihood would be compromised by Adam and his family if he were to refuse to have Meikal stay. They did not mind having him for a few nights as they believed him to be helpful with their youngest child and I had observed Meikal presented in ways to please and appease them. After we (social work) started to ask questions, Meikal himself began lining up another possible friend where he believed he would be welcomed. I was concerned this was due to the fear of going home but had to admire his problem-solving efforts. I wondered how much he had self-parented up to this point in his life.

THEORY: Identity

THEORY: Poverty

VALUES: Kindness

THEORY: Attachment patterns, social learning theory

THEORY: Self-efficacy

THEORY: Need, locus of control

The purpose of the visit we had today was to follow up on the initial conversations with Bianka about Meikal returning to her care, and the risks and safeguards around this. We needed to see if we could speak with her alone and to check the home conditions were safe.

Bianka let us in. Adam was there and put the dog in the kitchen again. I asked if Bianka and I could go through to a different room so we could hear each other as Rudi was frantically wanting to get out of the kitchen. I felt this was an opportunity to speak with Bianka alone. She agreed but Adam came too. I left this as I wanted to see how the conversation went first. I did not know the couple well and wanted to gain some rapport. I was conscious the evidence I had so far to enable me to assess risk was not enough to consider Meikal should not come back to his mother's care. Speaking with both Adam and Bianka would hopefully help me gather information.

THEORY: Empowerment

THEORY: Relational theory

I asked if Bianka had spoken with Meikal about coming home. She said he did not want to and was having a nice time with his friend. She also liked his friend's mum and sometimes helped her with her ironing. I repeated Bianka's legal responsibilities as a parent and clarified she understood this. I asked if Meikal was in contact with his father as perhaps he could care for him. Bianka immediately said Meikal's father had deserted them prior to his birth. This fitted with information Meikal had previously shared. I did not feel I should pursue this any further at this stage but considered I may return to it when speaking with Bianka alone.

THEORY: Social bonds

VALUES: Respect, anti-oppressive practice

I asked Bianka again what she thought the reason was that Meikal did not want to come home. She again said that he was having a nice time with his friend. I asked the same of Adam who said that he could not think of a reason and *'boys will be boys'*. I asked Adam how he felt about Meikal alleging that he (Adam) takes cocaine. I thought Adam gave a really good presentation of dismissing this, but his body language was tense and did not match the control he had in his voice. Bianka did not keep eye contact with me. It made me feel uneasy. This was still not enough evidence to suggest that Meikal should not return home, but I thought I was beginning to see more of how the family worked.

THEORY: Rational choice

I advised we would need to make further assessment of the situation for Meikal and reassured Bianka that there had never been a previous concern to my knowledge about her parenting of him to date. I said that we normally see parents separately as part of our assessments. I asked Bianka if she would be willing to come into the family centre to meet with me. Before she could speak, Adam said, *'You are welcome to come here but we are not coming to any office – Rudi has my back here.'*

VALUES: Transparency, integrity

THEORY: Power

My knees started to shake a bit, although Adam did not change his tone. I did not want him to see that I felt intimidated, so I said, *'I have dogs too. How's the training coming on?'* He spoke for a few minutes about Rudi, casually stating the dog's ability to *'bring a runner down'*. I felt this was intentionally to scare me. I thought about leaving but tried to appear as if I had not registered what he said. I tried to concentrate on the fact that I was there for a professional purpose to provide a service to Meikal. I led the conversation to joke about disobedient dogs I had had in the past to appear non-plussed. The support worker with

THEORY: Arousal–relaxation cycle

THEORY: Power

THEORY: Self-regulation

THEORY: Unconditional positive regard

me was looking decidedly edgy but I then asked to see round the house before I left 'as we normally do ask'. Adam showed me round and there were no concerns about the conditions. Meikal's room was suitable for a boy of his age.

I waited until I was near the front door in case I needed to leave quickly and let them know that we (Bianka, Adam and the social work department together) needed to make a decision about what to do next as Meikal could not stay indefinitely with his friend. I remarked that Rudi had now settled behind the kitchen door. I then said with some intended curiosity, 'Do you think that Meikal is scared of him? Is that why he does not want to come home?' Adam dismissed this saying, 'Rudi loves Meikal – they play like old pals.' Bianka dropped her gaze and did not look at me. I then asked, 'Do you think Meikal would be scared to come home for any other reason?' Adam smiled pleasantly and asked, 'What could he be scared of?' At the same time Bianka raised her eyebrows and made a face momentarily that sort of said 'well, you have seen what you have seen.' I said, 'I am not sure, but we need to come to some sort of solution. Can I ask, do you want him to come home Bianka?' She replied with a shrug, 'whatever is easiest, whatever he wants.'

I asked, 'Do you think it's better for him to be with his friends?' Bianka turned away quickly and brushed a tear out of her eye. She held her ground and said in a level voice, 'He's having a good time.' I made a mental note to ask Bianka more about the quality of her relationship with Meikal, prior to Adam coming into the family. It was clear I was not going to get to speak with Bianka on her own today. I was confident I had done the background checks for the family Meikal was currently with, so did not need to act differently to ensure his safety tonight.

I know that skilled abusers may never use violence against their intimate partners. I had evidence that Adam was controlling and to avoid placing any further strain on Bianka, I made to leave. I did not want to disempower her any more than it was clear she already was by Adam. I gave her my number and asked her to call me when it was convenient for us to come back so we could make a plan together.

Reflections

While I was in this house I was worried for myself and, of course, my colleague. This was a really uncomfortable visit. Even if I didn't know about Adam's family reputation, his presentation spoke volumes. He did not need to change his voice or do anything specific to be intimidating. It was really difficult to hold my authority and keep to a beginning, middle and end in the visit, when his body language was not congruent with his presentation. I knew I had to stick at it to do my job properly, but I was intimidated, for sure.

If I had not had my colleague with me I don't think I would have pushed to see round the house. I wanted to see if there was anyone else in there that they had not told us about and to get an idea of what Meikal's living conditions would be like if he returned. I did not expect to find evidence of drug misuse, but I looked round to observe and find out about their values and lifestyle. I thought I was gaining a reasonable picture of what it must be like to be a child living with Adam. I did think that Bianka was aware that she was disempowered and wondered if she had been trying to protect Meikal by letting him stay at friends. I wonder how Meikal's role and identity had been compromised when Adam arrived.

This visit was more assessment than intervention. To follow up, I think I need a discussion with Bianka on her own to see her more genuine position and the reasons she thinks Meikal is refusing to come home. If she sticks to what she has said already or shares more concerning information, we may have to find a more formalised temporary placement for Meikal and try and resolve the issues. Maybe Adam is scared that he will be homeless, as their house is in Bianka's name. *THEORY: Attribution*

VALUES: Dignity and respect

It is quite unusual for an 11-year-old child to tell people that he has 'left home' and I know I need to hear what he is communicating. I know what my gut feeling is saying too, and I am listening to it, but I need to know more so I can make a better assessment based on more evidence.

Reflective questions

- What could I have done differently to engage with Adam?

- What could I have done differently to engage with Bianka?

- What are Bianka's strengths?

- How have my frames of reference influenced my decision making?

- How can I effectively challenge the contradictions and keep the relationships?

- What would be different if I approached Adam thinking through the lens of trauma-sensitive practice?

Further reading

Ferguson, H (2011) *Child Protection Practice*. Basingstoke: Palgrave Macmillan.

Stark, E (2009) *Coercive Control: How Men Entrap Women in Personal Life*. New York: Oxford University Press.

Turney, D, Ward, A and Ruch, G (2018) *Relationship-based Social Work: Getting to the Heart of Practice*. London: Jessica Kingsley.

Walker, S (2012) *Effective Social Work with Children, Young People and Families: Putting Systems Theory into Practice*. London: Sage.

Case Study 8: Anna

Anna has been in care as a child and had been sexually abused by a male football coach who subsequently received a prison sentence for offences against her. Allegations she made against his friend were never proven. Anna retells graphic details of the abuse to anyone who will listen. She has received different services from a great number of workers over the years and yet her progress with recovery has not really begun. Professionals have not yet agreed on which diagnosis to use although Anna has been open to my Community Mental Health Team for about seven or so years. The current working diagnosis applied is post-traumatic stress disorder (PTSD). Anna uses an array of substances in no particular pattern and has no routine with sleep or food. Anna lives between four houses: her mother's house, her own house, her current partner's house, and her friend's squat. She refers to herself as a 'new age traveller'. Her baby, now ten months old, has been in the care of the local authority (LA) since he was born. Anna's other three children have been adopted.

THEORY: Recovery model

THEORY: Chaos

THEORY: Loss, trauma

When things do not go the way Anna wishes them to, she will climb up various high places in the town to place herself at risk. Police are then called. Invariably this results in Anna being taken by police to the local mental health hospital outpatients wing to be assessed. She has been subjected to various detention periods prior to the birth of her children, but mostly she has just been discharged. The police are exhausted with Anna's behaviour and losing patience with her.

We have held lots of multidisciplinary meetings with, and about, Anna. She is always invited to attend her meetings. Sometimes she arrives but sits outside the room as she wants to be around when she is being talked about but does not trust herself to manage her behaviour appropriately if she is triggered during the discussion. The team around her always facilitate this well as they are mindful of her presentation and background. We are now more ready for this than in the beginning. We now put a plastic

INTERVENTION: Empowerment

THEORY: Trauma

INTERVENTION: Unconditional positive regard, empowerment

VALUES: Respect, transparency, sensitivity

jug of water on the side table in the corridor but always remember to move the fire extinguisher to the inside of the door in case she attempts to throw it.

THEORY: Unconditional positive regard

VALUES: Honesty, integrity

INTERVENTION: Collaboration with others

THEORY: Emotional containment

VALUES: Authenticity, integrity, tolerance

Yesterday Anna came for her routine appointment with me. She has not attended the previous four appointments, so I was glad she came. My objective was to talk to her about managing her mental health and well-being. I could not ignore her drug use and needed to work alongside her drugs worker. I gave Anna the first ten minutes to 'decompress' and offload all the things that were on her mind. That meant that I validated her experiences and her views but did not agree with some of her values.

INTERVENTION: Schema therapy

THEORY: Abandonment

THEORY: Cognition, intelligence

INTERVENTION: Schema therapy

I reminded Anna of themes that we had previously talked about. I pointed to the obvious links between some of the material she was sharing and the abandonment schema she knew about. She could relate to the concepts and agreed that she perceived that people in her network might not be able or willing to continue to provide emotional support, connection or practical assistance. I was struck, in that moment, that the police and her baby's social worker were also responding in a rejecting and psychologically abandoning way towards Anna, but that her behaviour was provoking this response. Anna was stuck in a cycle. She also knew the theory. She was intellectually very able, but she was not able or willing to move from identifying patterns and making links to actually replacing habitual responses with healthier options that served her better in relationships and the community. I did not bring this into discussion in the session though, as the conversation was moving a pace. It has taken me more time to type it than to think it. That's just what happens I suppose – we can't always use our understanding in the moment, although we attempt to reflect *in* action.

VALUES: Maintaining boundaries

However, I was clear with Anna where I did not agree with her decision making but this did not bother her even slightly as she continued to talk rapidly. I drew her attention to her pressure of speech and advised her that I considered she may need some more help with managing her mental health. We had been in a similar place before, several times last year, and we had a relationship whereby Anna knew I could influence changes in her medication albeit I am not a prescriber. I would not say that this relationship was based on trust, but Anna could find my actions and my presentation predictable.

INTERVENTION: Pharmaceutical

VALUES: Reliability, non-judgemental

Anna was torn between wanting more or different medication and her perception of how this would 'look' to her son's social worker who had (legitimate) concerns that Anna's presentation was unstable. We spent some time talking about the possible risks and benefits of changing medication. I was very definite to work in an evidence-based way with Anna and referred to her previous presentation when on a different prescription. I proposed that she revisit some of the techniques we had taught her in group work, of distraction and grounding. Anna advised she and another service user were going to set up a private mindfulness class for people with mental health difficulties. I acknowledged this positively but did not pursue it as it was a distraction from the work we needed to do (and was also unrealistic). I reminded her of the distress tolerance techniques she knew about and, to check these were consolidated for her, I asked her a few questions around what she remembered. I mentioned the most recent incident on Thursday last week of when she could have used these techniques instead of climbing up the monument on Chapel Street.

INTERVENTION: Pharmaceutical

INTERVENTION: Motivational interviewing, opportunity-led practice

VALUES: Honesty, integrity, respect, ethical

INTERVENTION: Psycho-education

INTERVENTION: Dialectical behaviour therapy, self-regulation

INTERVENTION: Respectful challenge

Anna became defensive and was adamant that the 'police have a job to do' and 'it's up to them if they come or not.' I had heard her say this kind of thing many times. I was mindful of how fed up the police were of her behaviour and how they were looking for a resolution. I proposed to Anna that she may have been asking for help to regulate her emotions through her behaviour, and that if it was a person rather than a technique that she preferred I could suggest places to call 24 hours. Anna maintained that they do not listen, and in fact nobody listens. I proposed that we try calling a particular service together today in our session, so I could support Anna in how she might utilise this. Anna agreed but then immediately asked again for a change in prescription as she maintained this was the only thing that

THEORY: Defence mechanisms: Denial? Reaction formation?

THEORY: Trauma, abandonment, disorganised attachment

APPROACH: Coaching, nurturing, anti-oppressive, collaborative

INTERVENTION: Narrative therapy, counselling

did any good. I did not believe that medication was the only answer and considered that it may even have been masking some of her issues and impeding her recovery, although I could sense her pain in the moment. I tried to continue the conversation around stabilisation of her current substance use. Anna lost patience and stormed out. I was concerned that she was then likely to seek street drugs but also relieved that she had managed to leave without causing damage to the building or requiring police attendance.

Reflections

I feel sad that Anna's presentation is probably now so closely linked to her identity. She was so traumatised that I am not sure she would recognise her real self underneath all the defences and layers of protection she has developed. My assessment is that she has not actually matured through the stages into a consistent adult self, as her developmental trauma was so catastrophic. Her biological mother was emotionally unavailable to her and, in my view, it may have been that her mother also had unresolved trauma from her own childhood that she was unable to prevent impacting on Anna and her other children. If I didn't have my buffer of personal and professional protection – my support network, my learning and experience, and the ability to work with a close therapeutic alliance but still retain psychological self-preservation – I, for sure, would have succumbed to the sorrow and gravity of this case. Actually, maybe my self-preservation in this is to use the interventions I am familiar with and not to engage so much with the tragedy. I am OK up to a point with my professional use of self, if this is what is happening.

THEORY: Trauma

THEORY: Psychodynamic

THEORY: Life course, human development

THEORY: Trauma, attachment, defence mechanisms

THEORY: Trauma

THEORY: Resilience

THEORY: Grief

But is this enough? Prior to those thoughts, I was believing I am a bit lost with Anna as every intervention I have at my disposal has been tried. I feel we are just maintaining the status quo. I suppose it's good that she does keep checking in to appointments. I can't change the abandonment or abuse she experienced and how she is so easily triggered.

With someone like Anna, who is so demanding of professionals, it is easy to be drawn into thinking that the service has failed if change is not possible. I am clear that Anna is responsible for her own recovery. If workers claim success if a service user makes progress, they would then also have to claim responsibility if and when things deteriorated. I have had these conversations with members of the multidisciplinary team, and some of us have discussed how and what her behaviours trigger in us. (This has been quite informal though – I think we would benefit from team meetings devoting some time

THEORY: Self-determination

to discussing our resilience as workers within difficult cases.) I am also really aware that there is an undercurrent from another professional in the multi-agency group who does appear to be holding me responsible for change, which I am trying to manage as a side dynamic. I am not sure this person is aware of how she is coming across

and it may be a reflection of how disempowered she feels in her role. I am finding I need to justify my interventions quite explicitly with others knowing that this is around.

I know I need to just continue to offer Anna a service even if she is unable or unwilling to make the changes. She can and does use my service as a welcoming and dependable

base, and at one level maybe that is all she can engage with. We can be ready to respond when she is ready to progress in recovery, however she defines this. It would be clearer to assess her needs if she was not taking substances – we all know that. I will continue to assess her risk of suicide rather than assume she is maintaining a stable presentation of risk.

I am deeply saddened that the care system has let Anna down so badly and her sense of entitlement and lack of ability to self-regulate brings her to elicit care from emergency services. I need to try and work on well-being with

her, in the moment, like a solution-focused approach, which is really difficult when she is in crisis regarding her

wish to have her son returned to her care. I think she needs therapeutic re-parenting, but she has the autonomy to dis-

charge herself of course, if she does not like the direction of therapy. She has chosen to do this several times in the

past, basically because she is not ready. (I hold on to the hope that she will become ready.) She has also chosen to repeat skills-based courses, which is positive but has not brought change so far. I feel a little disheartened that I can't do more for her, but I have to reassure myself that my integrity is intact, even if I question my self-efficacy. If I learn different strategies, I will share them with Anna and of course I am not alone. My manager is supportive of my work and case decisions are jointly made.

Reflective questions

- How do I protect myself from feeling disempowered and deskilled?

- Do I really understand how to work with the shame this service user is experiencing?

- What personal trauma do I bring to this exchange and how can I guard against it impacting negatively on the service user and myself?

- What are the risks if I weigh having a good relationship more importantly than achieving change with the service user? Is it possible to do both?

- How would this situation look through a different lens?

- What would another worker do differently?

Further reading

De Shazer, S et al (2021) *More than Miracles: The State of the Art of Solution Focused Brief Therapy*. New York: Routledge.

McKay, M et al (2019) *The Dialectical Behaviour Therapy Skills Workbook*. Oakland, CA: New Harbinger Publications.

Rothschild, B (2010) *8 Keys to Safe Trauma Recovery*. New York: W W Norton.

Young, J E (2006) *Schema Therapy: A Practitioner's Guide*. New York: Guilford Press.

Case Study 9: Jimmy

There have been various concerns about Jimmy. Mostly these have related to his father's care of him. The family has a long history of intermittent social work involvement and, over the past couple of years, his mother has chosen to see him only once, albeit Jimmy lives three streets away from her. She has two much older children who are now young adults but who had been looked after in foster care for long periods in their earlier lives.

THEORY: Need

THEORY: Abandonment

THEORY: Early unmet need

As a baby, Jimmy had been looked after by his mother on her own, followed by a short period of care by his maternal grandmother and his mother together. His grandmother had sadly passed away and Jimmy and his mother moved to live with Jimmy's father. Jimmy had only lived with his mother and father together for a short time before he and his father, Bruce, had moved to a tenancy on their own. Jimmy was nearly two at that time. He is now 13 years old.

THEORY: Lack of secure base, loss and change, bereavement, early adversity

Today, Jimmy appeared in school with a black eye. He had been asked to speak with the headteacher in her office and told her that his father gave him the black eye on the door. Before the headteacher could say anything else, Jimmy began throwing things around her office, ripping books, upending the furniture and damaging the computer beyond repair. The headteacher had requested urgent assistance from other staff and the situation had been eventually de-escalated, without anyone injured.

THEORY: Attribution

THEORY: Arousal–relaxation cycle, de-escalation

The deputy headteacher had called me to inform of this incident. They had not experienced behaviour like this from Jimmy and were worried. They did not see any particular reason why he had reacted like this as he seemed calm when the headteacher initially spoke with him. I had asked that they keep him in the school for the rest of the afternoon as I needed to find out more about the black eye and how this had occurred. I could not get to the school immediately as I had a meeting, followed by a planned visit to another family. The deputy headteacher was reluctant to keep Jimmy and expected someone from social work to remove him from the school.

THEORY: Motivation, mindset?

INTERVENTION: Crisis intervention

VALUES: Inclusion, anti-oppressive practice

THEORY: Stigma

THEORY: Oppression, shame

THEORY: Identity, belonging

THEORY: Anti-oppressive practice

THEORY: Co-regulation, de-escalation

INTERVENTION: Relationship practice, nurture

THEORY: Self-regulation

VALUES: Collaboration, respect

INTERVENTION: Co-production

THEORY: Attachment, secure base

THEORY: Relationship practice

THEORY: Co-regulation

THEORY: Self-efficacy, group efficacy

VALUES: Integrity, authenticity, respect

THEORY: De-escalation, need

VALUES: Reliability, tolerance

In a similar situation with another child previously, I have been caught out with this – where schools expect social work to relieve them of issues by removing the child. I have come to the conclusion that I do not believe always removing a child from school is the solution for two reasons. First, that the child experiences stigma as they then are differentiated from their peers by someone coming to 'take them away'. This might have repercussions whereby the child is then a target for bullying. Second, the child has to re-enter the school to receive an education at a point in the future which can cause anxiety if they anticipate blaming and shaming on return. These can both impact their identity development. I believe that some reparation work can be done to mitigate this by the child receiving care and attention by well-regulated adults in the same environment, even if a break is then taken to consider options.

This approach obviously must be risk assessed and I spoke at length with the deputy headteacher asking more about the current situation, who Jimmy was with and how he was presenting. I do appreciate that schools do not have unlimited staff available for unspecified lengths of time without warning, but they do need to act as a secure base for children. I tried to strike a balance between appearing helpful and being firm that Jimmy stayed in the school.

I know Jimmy has a good relationship with senior staff. I have met them and shared professional decision making with them. I have seen them interact with Jimmy and I was comfortable with the level of risk in what I was asking. I felt that the staff needed to support each other to co-regulate and recognise that they had the professional capacity to manage. They had not needed to phone the police to contain Jimmy's behaviour during this incident. With care not to come across as patronising, I validated their position: that what they had done to de-escalate the incident was not easy, and Jimmy was lucky to have people around him who could support him to regain control of his behaviour. They were fully accepting that Jimmy could not go home until further discussion about his initial eye injury.

Once the deputy headteacher agreed that they would keep Jimmy in her office doing schoolwork until I arrived at 3pm, I was able to end the call and speak with my manager. I quickly updated him, and we agreed that I would ask Jimmy again how his black eye had happened and then decide if a brief discussion between the headteacher, the family protection department in the police, my manager and me was necessary to decide how best to respond. I would also try and find out what the trigger to the incident in school was and if the two things were connected in some way.

THEORY: Collaborative decision making

I was a bit worried that nobody had phoned Jimmy's dad and it did not seem right there had been a significant incident, yet he was unaware of this as a parent. I could reasonably justify this for an hour and a half and had planned with the deputy headteacher that we would discuss this when I met with them at the school.

VALUES: Integrity, trust, human rights? Ethical dilemma?

When I arrived there was no air of tension. I spoke with Jimmy in the presence of the deputy headteacher, firstly to check that he was OK and to ask him if he wanted to tell me all about what had happened as the teachers had been worried earlier. He shrugged and said, *'trashed Mrs Bowman's office'*. I left a pause, and he looked at the floor. I asked him to help me understand why this had happened. (I avoided saying directly, *'why did you do it?'* as I did not want him to feel shamed and refuse to communicate.)

Jimmy said, *'I want to go into care.'* I said, *'I am confused, Jimmy. What is making you say this? We have never discussed this before.'* I did not want to ask leading questions about his black eye, or make assumptions, as Jimmy may have needed to be more formally interviewed about this.

VALUES: Non-judgemental, sensitivity, respect

He said, *'Ryan is in care and he got a mountain bike with 18 gears. I want to go into care and get a motorbike.'* I knew Jimmy liked motorbikes as he was often down at the track watching what was going on. He had been quad-biking once with school too. I clarified his meaning and it turned out his dad had told him he did not have the money to buy Jimmy a

THEORY: Social constructionism, social learning

INTERVENTION: Opportunity-led

THEORY: Social bond theory, belonging, promoting resilience

INTERVENTION: Group work, solution focused

APPROACH: Asset-based, self-efficacy

VALUES: Self-determination, empowerment

APPROACH: Nurture

VALUES: Safety, partnership, dignity, sensitivity, empowerment

APPROACH: De-escalation

THEORY: Moral development

APPROACH: Collaboration

VALUES: Trust, integrity, role clarity

INTERVENTION: Task-centred practice

motorbike, so he thought that the way to get one was to go into care where the foster carers provide children with expensive items. Ryan and Jimmy had clearly talked about this. We had a conversation about how it did not follow that a child was looked after by a foster carer and then was given things, and that he lives with his dad. He said that his dad was 'boring', and so we chatted about other interests and groups that Jimmy might be able to join and how he might earn money to save up for a motorbike.

He touched his eye involuntarily and I said, '*That looks sore, what happened to you?*' He gave a plausible and genuine account (I believed) of running into a door. Shortly after, I made excuses and nipped out to call my manager. We agreed that Jimmy could go home, and I would take him there and explain what had happened to his dad.

I was conscious the deputy head had wanted Jimmy to have some time away from school to 'reflect on his behaviour' rather than come back tomorrow. I spoke with the headteacher separately who reluctantly agreed that he could come back the next day as normal. We both saw the need for Jimmy to make some sort of reparation and I suggested I speak with his dad about what this could look like. (I had no intention of speaking with Jimmy and his dad about criminal damage until the school were clearer on their position.)

It seemed that Jimmy was grateful he did not have to face his dad on his own. The conversation went OK, although Bruce was appropriately displeased. However, I did not think that Jimmy was at risk of harm. I was more concerned that Bruce had not put up a lockable cabinet like he had said he would for the two antique swords on the wall. He had recently won these in a bet and Jimmy and a friend had been found playing with them a couple of weeks ago. Bruce had been annoyed with him but did not see the level of risk I saw. Nobody was hurt. However, Bruce had agreed to get a cabinet nonetheless, which he had not done. I had asked him to store the swords in a safe place until this could be done, yet on today's visit, there they were – still on the wall next to a horrible model (my personal view) of a wrestling figure on a motorbike.

I challenged him about the swords, and he took them down saying he would deal with it. Although it had irritated me that he had dismissed my advice, I thought it best to visit again soon and check that he had followed through with it this time, rather than labour the point there and then.

THEORY: Unconditional positive regard

APPROACH: Collaboration, de-escalation

I checked out Bruce's version of how Jimmy got his black eye which was consistent with Jimmy's story. We talked about taking responsibility. Then we agreed that I would phone the school to suggest that Jimmy write a letter of apology to Mrs Bowman for his behaviour today. Jimmy was in a good mood when I left, albeit not keen to offer to do some tidying up duties around the school by way of reparation.

THEORY: Moral development, reparation, integrity

Reflections

I am aware that I am Jimmy's sixth social worker, and I don't think I have been able to connect well with him. This has been a challenging case as the issues are different each time there is an incident. There is no pattern, and no real consistent escalation. Each time the issues and concerns can be brought to a tolerable risk level. His father has some unhelpful values but, with guidance, is generally providing for Jimmy's needs.

I always find it interesting how we respond to fathers who are raising children alone. I have been keen to approach my role as a statutory social worker for Jimmy looking through the lens of good parenting, rather than gendered parenting. Maybe it has been wrong to do that. The dilemma is that there is no evidence just now of an impact on Jimmy of Bruce's lifestyle, but his values may impact longer term. I wonder if Jimmy is a bit embarrassed about his father sometimes, and this was why he thought it would be more fun in care.

VALUES: Non-discriminatory, non-judgemental, empowerment, respect, inclusion, equality

However, just because I do not like some of the values and interests that Bruce has does not make them illegal. Bruce is managing his role as a parent, and to his credit, he could have become really annoyed with Jimmy for damaging property at the school, but he did not.

VALUES: Respecting diversity

I thought about the incident. I realised that I was wrong initially. Jimmy did not need anyone to help him self-regulate; he had in fact been in control all the way along. His outburst and destructive behaviour was planned with clear motive rather than reactive violence. He had every opportunity to make a false allegation against his father (with regards the black eye) to achieve his goal, but he did not. I think we should take this at face value.

THEORY: Social bonds?

VALUES: Non-judgemental, inclusion

I want to avoid a 'reintegration meeting' where Jimmy has to talk about his behaviour and experience over-shaming. I hope I can influence the school into accepting an apology letter.

THEORY: Shame

VALUES: Empowerment, inclusion

Reflective questions

- Should I have discussed the injury with Jimmy's dad first before taking him home?

- How do I manage my own emotions when triggered?

- What are the dominant discourses in this context and what is the construct of the problem?

- What are the unspoken challenges within these different relationships?

- What are this family's assets?

- What should be the planned outcomes in this case and how can we measure success?

Further reading

Bomber, L M and Perry, A (2020) *Know Me to Teach Me: Differentiated Discipline for Those Recovering from Adverse Childhood Experiences*. London: Worth Publishing.

Butler, G (2013) *Observing Children and Families Beyond the Surface*. Northwich: Critical Publishing.

Gibbs, J C (2019) *Moral Development and Reality: Beyond the Theories of Kohlberg, Hoffman, and Haidt*. New York: Oxford University Press.

Horwath, J (2013) *Child Neglect – Planning and Intervention*. Basingstoke: Palgrave Macmillan.

Case Study 10: Rosella

Rosella is a 63-year-old woman of Romanian heritage. She was born in the UK and had a family of eight children. Her husband passed away a few years ago. She lives in a caravan on the LA caravan site on the edge of town. She is registered as disabled due to mobility issues. She uses a wheelchair when she leaves the caravan, which is very infrequently. Someone has made her a little shed for her wheelchair at the side of the caravan.

THEORY: Loss, bereavement, change

Unfortunately (the same person, maybe) made her some kennels and Rosella previously had significant issues with the number of animals she kept. When my team first became involved with Rosella, due to her mental health concerns about three years or so ago, they had needed to promptly work with animal services to rehome several dogs. Two needed to be euthanised.

THEORY: Attachment, emotions, need

THEORY: Loss, bereavement, change

Rosella has one little terrier dog at the moment. His name is Stanley. She puts him out the back caravan steps on a long extendable lead to go to the toilet. Neighbours constantly complain about this as she does not clean up after him. She has had several visits from environmental health workers. She also has about seven cats who come and go from the caravan through a window which Rosella insists on leaving open, although she has been advised about security. She does not acknowledge her vulnerability.

THEORY: Need

THEORY: World view

Until a week ago, Charlene, who identifies as Rosella's daughter, was going in and helping Rosella. Charlene is not a biological daughter, but someone whom Rosella brought into her family, informally, during her childhood. Charlene has just had a diagnosis of a life-limiting condition. She has decided that she will step back from her caring role for Rosella. This places Rosella in a vulnerable position.

THEORY: Loss, change

It has just come to light that there are young men in their early 20s in the nearby caravans that Rosella has relied on in the past couple of weeks to bring her shopping and cigarettes. I worry that the young men may be aware that Rosella is in receipt of a reasonable amount of money, and she is giving her bank card to them. The dilemma is that she has capacity to decide to do this, yet it is unwise.

THEORY: Self-determination

Today I needed to visit Rosella to discuss other, more formal supports she could utilise. My relationship with Rosella is not strong. I have been involved with her off and on in my role as her community mental health worker. I knew today was going to be difficult because Rosella is wary of those who she perceives as authority figures.

THEORY: Need

THEORY: Dependency

THEORY: Assumptive world, social constructionism

I proposed to her that I thought it was risky giving her bank card to the young men and that we needed to think about a different way to approach this. I suggested that she got a taxi to the supermarket herself for her shopping, but she thought that Charlene could get her list when she got her own shopping and send it round in a taxi to her. Rosella was not willing to pay for the taxi, however. If she had not got Charlene, she said she would rely on the boys, Ricky and Tam, who would 'come anyway'. This made me suspicious, but I said nothing.

THEORY: Denial, entitlement

THEORY: Anxiety, arousal–relaxation cycle

THEORY: Self-regulation

I confirmed that Rosella knew that Charlene was quite unwell, but this did not seem to deter her from thinking that Charlene was really obliged to come and support her as '*she is younger*' and '*I did it for her.*' This pushed my buttons, for sure, as Rosella was being quite insensitive and entitled when Charlene was more vulnerable than she herself was. I told myself to breathe in and out.

THEORY: Need

THEORY: Risk, need

I advised Rosella that we needed to prioritise how she was going to get her medication and asked what she thought. She said that when the time came, she would pay Ricky to go and get it. I am glad I asked as this confirmed what I thought she might do. I did not want the young men anywhere near this medication as it is a controlled drug. I was clear about this to Rosella and the risks that were around for her if she missed her medication. She was aware of this and mumbled something dismissive to me.

Instead, I suggested that we could look into her medication being delivered and she agreed. I tried to make a couple of phone calls to her own doctor and pharmacy but neither answered their phones. Rosella said, *'See, nobody wants to know. I will deal with it myself.'* I assured her that I would follow this up and give her the information so that she could sign up for the delivery service. I felt sure that she would be prioritised for this service and made a mental note to speak with the pharmacy about not permitting the collection of this prescription by anyone other than Rosella – or Charlene if she ended up agreeing to do it one more time. (I would let Rosella and Charlene discuss this between them if they chose to and didn't draw attention to this as a possibility.)

THEORY: Self-efficacy? Denial? Locus of control?

VALUES: Collaboration

I said that we could also look into getting a volunteer to get Rosella her shopping. She became agitated saying that she did not need this if Charlene *'pulled her weight and was not so selfish'*. She told me to *'go talk to her'*. I had reiterated that Charlene had done really well, when she was obviously ill, prior to her diagnosis. I reminded her that Charlene had come round every day and cleared up the dog poo and did other things for Rosella. Although I was triggered by Rosella's insistence that Charlene should prioritise Rosella's needs above her own, I did recognise that Rosella was experiencing loss and this was not easy for her.

THEORY: Anxiety, arousal–relaxation cycle, loss and change

THEORY: Denial, entitlement, loss and change?

VALUES: Integrity, respect

VALUES: Non-judgemental, sensitivity

Early on in my involvement with Rosella I had asked about her children. This topic had proved very difficult for her and she had had a significant episode of mental ill-health shortly after this. I avoided speaking about her children today for that reason. I did not consider mentioning her probable loss of Charlene.

THEORY: Trauma

INTERVENTION: Trauma-informed

VALUES: Sensitivity

I reiterated that we needed to help Rosella stay safe, and that it would not be good if Ricky or Tam took her bank card and did not return it, so we needed to sort a proper arrangement with someone else. I said that if her bank card was not returned it takes a while to get another one and that it would put her in a difficult situation not having access to money. Knowing how she is fixated on smoking, I recognised that she accepted this.

THEORY: Risk and need

THEORY: Disempowerment

INTERVENTION: Opportunity led

INTERVENTION: Crisis management

I much preferred an organised formal approach to getting her shopping rather than consider anyone else in Rosella's or Charlene's own networks. Not that I am risk averse, more that I have heard them speak of people and have drawn conclusions that it would probably not go well. I also saw that it would be really difficult to unpick an arrangement with some of the people in their network once it got established and there may be risk to Rosella along the way. This would also take a lot of energy on my part (and frankly, I have more to do).

Rosella said, 'You better not send that Grace!' Grace was Rosella's social worker before me. Rosella had not liked her and openly said that was because she was black. This had been a real dilemma for them at the time and had been talked about in team supervision. Grace had been well

THEORY: Empowerment, emotions, locus of control

supported by us all and by Rhona, our manager, but in the end, it had been Grace's decision to move from the case.

VALUES: Integrity, inclusion, respecting diversity, human worth, authenticity, anti-oppression

This sat really uneasily with me, that Rosella had blocked the service previously, on the grounds of race. I had had to dig fairly deep to bring myself to work with unconditional

THEORY: Humanistic

positive regard towards Rosella at the start. I thought this would fade over time as I got to know her, but it had not.

I simply said, 'Grace is a qualified social worker, with more experience and knowledge than most of us have. Grace is not a volunteer. I will put a service application into the volunteer centre when I get back to the office, though.' And I thought, 'you will take the volunteer for their kindness, whatever their background and colour of their skin.' I hope

THEORY: Self-regulation

VALUES: Tolerance

that I kept my tone unchanging and that my real thoughts did not come through.

VALUES: Trust

I needed to wrap up the visit positively so that I could retain the threads of our relationship and continue to work with Rosella. I was aware that I had not directly talked much about her current mental health but thought that dealing with more pressing things would support this indirectly.

INTERVENTION: Solution-focused brief therapy

I had often worked in a more solution-focused way with Rosella, to get ahead of any precipitating factors which might impact her mental health so this approach would not have been unusual to her.

I had ruled out narrative approaches quite early on with Rosella, as I figured that it would only encourage her to fabricate stories which would confuse my assessment of her needs. She still offered stories regularly, but I had learned how to redirect her once I got to know her a bit. However, today I took a cue from the dog and encouraged her to speak about him when he was younger. I thought that his presence relaxed Rosella and that he was a protective factor in her life. She told me a couple of stories about him and how he had been with the rest of 'the pack' (the other dogs before they were rehomed).

INTERVENTION: Narrative therapy

I said, *'So what have you got planned for the rest of the day?'* to ground her after our conversation. She replied that she was going to clean the kitchen and crochet a hat for Stanley. When I left, she said something quite negative as a parting shot, that I recognised was a line from a film. I smiled gently and pretended to ignore it, saying that I would contact her either today or tomorrow.

THEORY: Unconditional positive regard

Reflections

THEORY: Self-efficacy

When I left, I was kicking myself – I should have explored online shopping options with Rosella. I know she can work internet banking so she could probably be taught how to do online grocery shopping. I can suggest this when I call her back. Internet shopping might work against her recovery though so I will have to be careful about promoting isolation. I think I allowed myself to be distracted by all the other feelings that this visit was bringing.

THEORY: Inclusion, marginalisation

My thoughts were mainly underpinned with the sense that Rosella thought she was entitled. My personal beliefs are that she could do more for herself and that her reliance on Charlene had become a convenience rather than an actual need. Rosella has the ability to do more for herself and is making choices not to. I figure it is just motivation and mindset again. And values – I suppose that is the nub of it: our values are so far apart. I felt really triggered by her entitled presentation, her arrogance and her long-standing racist attitude.

THEORY: Normative need

THEORY: Learned helplessness, rational choice

THEORY: Motivation, behavioural drivers, emotions, world view

THEORY: Fixed mindset, world view, attachment and loss?

INTERVENTION: Anti-oppressive practice

I know it is my job to empower people, and I can normally work with people to help them overcome barriers. I wonder where theories of learned helplessness sit alongside personalisation agendas. I am all for promoting resilience and helping people live a fulfilling life of course, but preference is different to need.

THEORY: Empowerment, resilience, satisfaction, equality

THEORY: Normative need

INTERVENTION: Empowering, validating, unconditional positive regard

I think I did well to finish off this conversation with Rosella in a way in which she felt validated, but I am uncomfortable with the incongruence I felt. I acknowledge (to you privately) that I don't actually like Rosella and am holding onto techniques and training rather than working with emotional authenticity. I worry that I am overly optimistic about risk because I am trying to seem unfazed and supportive.

THEORY: Cognitive dissonance

THEORY: Rule of optimism

Reflective questions

- What could be some other explanations for Rosella's behaviours?

- How is it possible to work with someone you have personally no time for?

- What are the ethics around the themes raised in this story?

- What deeper reflections would be helpful for me to discuss in supervision?

- What are Rosella's assets in her current situation?

- What other services and community connections might be appropriate to link with?

Further reading

Bartoli, A (ed) (2013) *Anti-racism in Social Work Practice*. St Albans: Critical Publishing.

Brown, K (2010) *Vulnerable Adults and Community Care*. Exeter: Learning Matters.

Machin, L (2013) *Working with Loss and Grief*. London: Sage.

Mantell, A and Scragg, T (2018) *Reflective Practice in Social Work*, 5th ed. London: Learning Matters.

Case Study 11: Becky

I was asked to visit a family who were not known to social work. The child, Becky (aged seven), had told her teacher that her brother, Sean (aged ten), had locked her in the shed, pinged elastic bands at her through the 'high up window' and then left her there until it was dark. When she was telling her teacher, Becky was reportedly 'inconsolable', which was out of character. She would not say 'where mummy was' when this had happened.

I looked up the electronic recording system to see if there was any other information. Other than two food parcels given a year or so ago there was no information about any of the family members. I asked the school for more information on Sean and they advised he was a bit outspoken in class and his attendance was at 90 per cent (compared to 99 per cent for Becky). He always seemed to have a lot of friends and handed in homework every week though.

I needed to visit to see what sense the family made of Becky's allegation and to assess if further intervention was needed. On the first visit, I didn't want to speak with Becky's mum, Mandy, when either of the children were there as I didn't know what actual risk we were managing and what reception we would get. I wanted to de-escalate things where I could, and help Mandy avoid feelings of shame and panic in front of the children. We chose a time when the children were confirmed to be in school. As this was an unknown family, I took a colleague with me.

> THEORY: Attribution
>
> THEORY: Need
>
> THEORY: Shame and resilience, arousal–relaxation cycle
>
> INTERVENTION: Anti-oppressive practice

Mandy answered the door and I said that we had some information that she would want to know about. She let us in and I outlined what Becky had told her teacher. At first Mandy dismissed the allegation, saying that Becky had a lively imagination and was making it up. I didn't pursue further questioning around this. I asked who else lived in the house. Mandy said that it was *just the three of us*. I noticed a care home uniform hanging up and commented *'Oh do you work at Firtree? Is it shift work you do?'* Mandy confirmed it was and got agitated saying that they were all fine and we could leave now, and she would have a word

> VALUES: Honesty, sensitivity
>
> THEORY: Arousal–relaxation cycle

with Becky for making things up. I said that social work were there to help rather than make things difficult and we needed to make sure people are safe. She snapped, *'Well I will just phone in sick then so I can watch them both like a hawk – I will lock all the doors so they can't even go outside! Satisfied?'* She made to move to show us out. We got up and I said quietly, *'We are here to help Mandy. What can we do, after we leave here, that would be helpful?'* She burst into tears and said, *'You can't help – not unless you have £4,500 to give me!'* My colleague asked, *'Why do you need £4,500?'* She then let us know about the debt her ex-husband had left her with and how she needed to work to pay this off. I asked, *'Who looks after the children when you are at work, Mandy?'* She was very vague, saying *'friends'* and would not confirm who – but asked us again tartly to leave. I said that we needed to make sure that she had adequate childcare when she went to work and she shouted, *'nobody will have him!'* We clarified that she meant that the after school club had asked Sean not to return and that she had limited choice of reliable friends. I asked if there were times that the children were on their own. She said, *'they are not on their own, Polly [a neighbour] can see them from her window until I get home'* – she then softened and began sobbing saying, *'I don't know what to do.'* She agreed that she needed reliable childcare. We stayed until we had talked about options of other after school care arrangements and she agreed to call her boss to advise on the shifts in the coming week that she could not do due to having no childcare. I agreed to making a referral to 'Welfare Rights' to see what could be done to maximise her income and manage the debt.

I asked Mandy if there were other times that Sean might have not been kind to Becky and she went on to describe some behaviour that she found challenging. I asked if she knew what the behaviour was 'all about'. I asked in this way as it was less challenging or patronising to her as a parent. In transactional analysis terms, I wanted to relate to her adult to adult. She said things had been difficult since her husband had left. Sean was angry and blamed her for his father leaving and that they had not got any money to spend

Margin annotations:

VALUES: *Integrity, empowerment*

THEORY: *Arousal–relaxation cycle*

THEORY: *Poverty*

THEORY: *Oppression, loss and change, ambiguous loss, transitions*

THEORY: *Of rational choice*

VALUES: *Social justice*

VALUES: *Sensitivity*

THEORY: *Transactional analysis, relationship theory*

THEORY: *Loss and change, identity? Role confusion?*

THEORY: *Attribution*

anymore. She said he was acting out as his dad does not get in contact. She was agreeable for me to 'find a worker who is not a social worker' who had 'done this kind of thing before' for Mandy to 'pick her brains' about how to manage Sean's behaviours.

THEORY: Shame, stigma, loss of the assumptive world, identity development

INTERVENTION: Anti-oppressive language, communication

Mandy seemed like she was engaging and open enough to acknowledge she was struggling. I wanted to talk about strengths to lift her mood. Without belittling her I wanted to find a way of helping her to see her own strengths. I actually felt quite sorry for her. She was under a lot of pressure and had not, at face value, reached this situation through her own decision making or poor judgement, although I did not know much about her husband or what had happened in their relationship. I did not know anything about his parenting values other than that he had abandoned his family. Now was not the time to get into that. I turned the conversation to Sean's strengths, asking what he likes to do when he is not at school. Mandy spoke about Sean having outgrown his bike and not having the money to go to the sports centre like they used to or go to see the ice hockey. In fact, she said, they do nothing nice now.

THEORY: Empowerment

VALUES: Respect, ethical practice, collaboration

THEORY: Empowerment

VALUES: Compassion

INTERVENTION: Strengths-based practice

I spoke about some of the free stuff I knew was happening in the town, and the free holiday clubs. She seemed interested. I said that we had asked the school how Sean was and they had said he has plenty of friends. I smiled and suggested that he must be 'good fun'. Mandy agreed that he could be. I said 'You know, the school don't have any other concerns apart from what Becky said – so you must be doing OK [she understood this to mean OK as a parent] – you are meeting their needs – you have a lovely house, the kids do their homework – it just sounds like you are not having such a good time and are under some stress to get everything to come together. To me it seems like you have come a long way, although of course I don't know the half of it.' Tears welled up in her eyes. I actually wanted to hug her but stopped myself. I had allowed myself to be triggered by the injustice of the position she had been put in. Instead, I said one of our workers would speak to her some more about 'getting back on track'.

THEORY: Need

VALUES: Professional boundaries

I said that when we visit families, we usually ask to see the children's bedrooms. Mandy was agreeable for this and we had some light-hearted exchange about the mess children make. Mandy's house looked like children lived there but there were no concerns about this – there would have been concerns if it had been too tidy. Just before leaving I asked, *'what are you going to do about Becky – she was right to tell the teacher. How will you handle it when she comes home?'* Mandy said more calmly that she would talk to her. *'And Sean?'* Mandy said that she would *'try – depending on what mood he is in'*. We agreed that I would give her a ring at the end of the week and she willingly gave her phone number.

THEORY: Empowerment and self-efficacy

We left satisfied that Mandy saw the issues and the risks and that she was enabled to pursue solutions. I advised Mandy I would tell the school that we had spoken together, and the children were fine to come home from school as usual. I was aware that this was not all the work we needed to do but was comfortable that the groundwork had been prepared on this first visit.

THEORY: Empowerment

INTERVENTION: Language of partnership working

Reflections

If I had challenged Mandy when she had said that Becky was making things up I think it would have been more difficult to get to the point where she told us the issues and we were able to work out risks. I was careful of my demeanour throughout to keep my body language open and approachable. I was conscious that I needed to regulate my emotions to help Mandy regulate hers and the underlying belief might be that we were there to take her children away, even if that was not explicitly discussed.

THEORY: Power and communication

If I had pursued the fact that I thought Becky was telling the truth and demanded an explanation from Mandy, this would have been punitive and risked non-engagement. For me, this was not an option. I could see that this was a situation where early intervention could benefit. Granted I had made no assessment of the attachment of the children but Mandy spoke like she cared about them and there was nothing in the home that made me concerned that they were not provided for. If there had been, I might have asked some different questions. I had timed the request to see the bedrooms until after we had gained a bit of rapport and Mandy was less defensive. I specifically did not ask to look in their fridge as the concerns raised were not about the children presenting as hungry. I figured that we could pick up on Sean's challenging behaviour at school another day, if needed. The school were not very concerned in that respect and he was achieving alongside his peers. I was confident that a support worker could gain a relationship with the family, see how the family systems worked and we could then make a fuller assessment of risk and need.

VALUES: Ethical practice, anti-oppression

VALUES: Empowerment

THEORY: Need

THEORY: Protective factors and assessment of resilience

VALUES: Ethical practice, collaboration

THEORY: Ecological, systems

I am not convinced that Mandy won't rely on Polly to oversee the children from her window again, but I had to take her word (on this visit) that she was going to sort more appropriate childcare. She did see it as her responsibility to sort out. I was relieved that the situation was not more serious, but of course it was serious from Becky's point of view. I should have discussed with Mandy how the school could support Becky (and Sean), without undermining her role as their mother, but this would be a reason to follow up

THEORY: Locus of control

THEORY: Shame, identity

VALUES: Integrity,
anti-oppression

by phone and check that she has made arrangements with work until childcare can be sorted. I was prepared to help her further as I realise it is not easy or straightforward.

I thought I had done OK with gaining her trust and trying to boost her self-esteem. I thought that the rapport I had gained with her might make it easier for her to trust the support workers. Although I don't often think about that, now I have come to reflect, if we have an interaction with a service user that does not go well, it does make it more difficult for the next worker to gain trust. We may see ourselves as beginning a new relationship with a service user, but they may carry the perceptions of, and possibly mistrust of, a whole long succession of workers. So, a new worker is not really beginning from a completely fresh starting point with some people, even if we, ourselves, experience the relationship as new. Food for thought.

Reflective questions

• What do I need to know more about?

• Have I been perceived as non-judgemental and compassionate?

• How have my frames of reference influenced my decision making?

• How do I know this person understood the risk and was able to take action?

• Have I found the balance between facilitating, supporting, advocating and directly intervening?

• Have I used professional authority appropriately?

Further reading

Escudero, V and Friedlander, M L (2017) *Therapeutic Alliances with Families: Empowering Clients in Challenging Cases*. Cham, Switzerland: Springer.

Frost, N, Abbot, S and Race, T (2015) *Family Support: Prevention, Early Intervention and Early Help*. Cambridge: Polity.

Pincus, L and Dar, C (1980) *Secrets in the Family*. London: Faber.

Seyderhelm, A (2019) *Helping Children Cope with Loss and Change*. London: Routledge.

Case Study 12: Mattias

Mattias is a 26-year-old man, currently resident within a locked ward which operates with quite a rigid structure. He has been there for about ten weeks and developed some tentative, superficial relationships with other residents. He is very polite to them but visibly wary. He chooses to spend long periods in his room.   — *THEORY: Trauma*

Mattias was eight years old when his mother died by suicide. He had been physically and emotionally abused over several years by the people his mother had left him with. Mattias had spent his teenage years in various foster care placements and latterly residential and secure care. He had developed issues with polysubstance use and had been admitted to hospital on several occasions for emergency treatment due to this. Three times he had nearly died. He has acquired brain injury due to substance use. Prior to this, it had been queried whether Mattias may have met the criteria for diagnosis of a personality disorder. However, this could not be established due to the impact of his continued substance use. Mattias has co-ordination problems with his left arm, and he becomes frustrated and agitated. He does not like to be in crowded places. He has had some panic attacks which he can recall vividly.   — *THEORY: Bereavement*   — *THEORY: Self-regulation*

Mattias spends a lot of time in his day ticking off the hours in his notebook. He periodically wishes to die and will date and time his intent to end his life in his notebook. Staff have attempted to track the triggers for this, but they can't yet be consistently patterned. Mattias tolerates being placed under constant observation and will interact with one staff member at a time, provided they are at a distance.   — *INTERVENTION: Suicide intervention*

I have been working with and for Mattias for around a year and during this time he has begun to relax in my company. He has been detained several times and appears to settle in a closed environment where he interestingly appears relieved when free from substances. He continues to refuse an advocate and requests bulletproof glass in his window, however.   — *INTERVENTION: Relationship-based practice*   — *THEORY: World view*

THEORY: Empowerment

My visit to Mattias today was to speak with him ahead of a review meeting that is scheduled later this week. Mattias has got capacity to make his own decisions and it is really important he is central to the discussion. However, Mattias

APPROACH: Anti-oppressive

is refusing to go as he does not like being in a room full of people. I considered my role to empower Mattias in ways

THEORY: Trauma

that would reduce his distress.

Firstly, I spoke with the ward staff to understand how Mattias was presenting today and to ask their views on how he might be enabled to take part in his meeting. I figured it would be easy for some colleagues to reduce Mattias, in the discussion, to a cluster of symptoms and so

THEORY: Empowerment, complexity theory

APPROACH: Humanistic

I was keen to ensure his voice was heard.

The nurse advised there was no change. Mattias was still saying he was not attending his review. I did not suggest the attendees of the meeting came to meet Mattias where he was as I knew the rigid structure of the department would not allow for that. I suggested to the nurse that

APPROACH: Enabling

Mattias might want to enter the room first and for other people to enter one by one slowly and sit at a pre-agreed distance from him. The nurse suggested Mattias could take a pillow so he could put it round his ears if he wanted to block out the voices. I was not sure how productive this would be if we wanted Mattias to participate in the conversation.

APPROACH: Enabling

I asked if Mattias could attend over a digital platform, so he could be supported to join the discussion in his room by one person, if he was overwhelmed by people. The nurse was not so sure this could be arranged as they did not have a device and the one-to-one support time would need to be agreed with her senior.

I went to speak with Mattias. When I had first met him, it was a bit of a surprise that he constantly takes off his jumper and t-shirt during conversations rather than sitting still not doing anything. As his muscle co-ordination is not so good, this is a struggle and, for someone who does not know him, there would be the temptation to ask if he would like some help. However, Mattias clearly does not wish for any help. When he has taken these clothes off, he attempts to fold them and places his glasses on top. He then puts them on again and repeats. It was no different today and I was mindful to keep my voice quite monotone so as not to agitate him.

> APPROACH: Trauma-informed
> THEORY: Communication

As I was with Mattias, the nurses paused their regular checks on his well-being. I asked him how he was doing, and he said he did not like Janine (another resident) who looks at him funny when he is eating. Otherwise, he said he was OK. He then immediately asked if he could have more medication and if this could be discussed at the forthcoming meeting. I said he could raise this with his psychiatrist in the meeting and that we would also discuss his longer-term care too. He asked me if I would ask on his behalf as he would not be coming.

> THEORY: Group dynamics?

> THEORY: Request for advocacy

I was a little worried that in a previous meeting, I had observed Mattias' psychiatrist almost putting words in the person's mouth. The psychiatrist did most of the talking about his understanding of the person's presentation and did not get a clear perspective straight from the person herself by asking the right questions. The person ended up staying on the ward when I believed she was ready for discharge. I was aware my colleague, Fran, had raised a formal complaint about this psychiatrist in another similar situation. With this in mind, I was really keen to ensure Mattias was offered the chance to present his own situation. There were some thoughts in the multidisciplinary team about moving Mattias to a closed rehabilitation centre for people who had brain injury, although there were no firm views. He really needed to be part of these discussions.

> THEORY: Power

> THEORY: Oppression

> APPROACH: Anti-oppressive practice

> INTERVENTION: Residential care

I said to him it would be better if he could describe to the people at the meeting how he felt and any worries he had. He became agitated, wandering around the room naked from the waist up. He said that he would have no worries if he were dead, and that death would be the 'calmest he could ever be'. He said he did not want to be a mess and if he could just stay here and have more of his specified medication, he would be no trouble for anyone. He muttered something which indicated worries about moving on.

> THEORY: Arousal–relaxation cycle

VALUES: Trust, sensitivity,
authenticity, non-judgemental

APPROACH: Recovery
orientation

THEORY: Assumptive world,
culture shock

—I talked for a bit about the limitations of his stay in this ward and he was doing well with his recovery goals. I spoke about the changes in his presentation compared to several weeks ago. I noted it would not be good to stay in a place like this for a long time as, for one thing, he might find it more difficult to settle back into his house when he was discharged.

Mattias put his clothes on and asked if the nurses had told me when he was going to die. I said they had not mentioned this. He said he would wait until he heard what everyone said at the meeting and then decide. He said, '*And you have been really helpful to me – you're one of the good ones. When I do die, you can have all the coins I have in the special tomato soup can in my kitchen: last cupboard on the left, right at the back. It's got a false bottom – just twist. You'll see. You deserve it – it's my secret stash. You can spend it how you want. I won't ask.*'

VALUES: Integrity, authenticity,
empowerment

APPROACH: Ethics discussion?

THEORY: Resilience

—I said this was a really kind thought, and good to hear that I had been helpful to him, but that I could not accept the coins as we could not take gifts from people we are here to help. I also said it was positive that he believed that he could wait to live to hear the outcome of the meeting. He said that I could tell 'the boss' he would be fine staying here if he could give him more meds. (He meant the psychiatrist.)

APPROACH: Person-centred

I agreed that medication could be on the list of things to discuss at the meeting but said that I was thinking more about other things that would need to be talked about – what was important to him moving forward and what he wanted to happen next. I said I was there to support but it would be really good if we could find a way for him to find the courage to tell it like it is – to tell people what they don't know.

THEORY: Enabling

THEORY: Arousal–relaxation
cycle

—I suggested that I could try and source a device that could link him electronically to the meeting and perhaps he and I could sit in this room and join the meeting from a distance. This triggered him to jump up and pace around again, with t-shirt half off and his arm moving about in an uncontrolled manner. He did not want a device in his room in case 'people' tried to contact him. We quickly abandoned this idea. I explored some other options to facilitate his attendance, but he seemed to be making a rational choice not to attend as he perceived he would become distressed and panic. He told me that it was his right and his decision not to attend. He said that people would think he was weird and lock him up forever. He said he could not trust himself not to be weird and they better not send him to a group for weird people.

THEORY: Distorted cognitions?

INTERVENTION: Emotional intelligence, de-escalation

THEORY: Rational choice

THEORY: Locus of control

I reassured him and took notes about his preferences for the future and that he wanted Amanda (the neuro-physiotherapist) to visit him again to 'remind him what to do'. I emphasised to him that I would share his views and agreed to give him a call on the morning of the meeting to check out that he still felt the same or if his views had changed. I told him I would come by and see him straight after the meeting too. We chatted about his writings on his notepad, and I suggested he could ask the nurses for some more art paper and soft pencils. He was calm and I handed over to the nurses to ensure they resumed their check levels.

APPROACH: Trauma-informed, person-centred

APPROACH: Empowering

THEORY: Advocacy

Reflections

VALUES: Honesty, trust, integrity, dignity, sensitivity

I don't believe I could have done much else to reduce the power imbalances and encourage Mattias to attend his meeting. Any more suggestions and I would have been verging on being oppressive and coercive. I will work within the systems and the competence around him, to make sure that I put in place what I can to support his rights. As well

APPROACH: Dignity

as working within a human rights perspective, I needed to help reduce distress in the moment for Mattias so as not to set his recovery back – this dilemma is a difficult balance with him. I suppose if Mattias is not speaking for himself, I can advocate for him in a way that ensures a more balanced discussion with the psychiatrist. I need to find out more about the proposals for a bed at the rehabilitation centre and hear what the multidisciplinary team are saying

INTERVENTION: Solution-focused

before supporting Mattias in a more solution-focused way. I am hoping it can all be a very planned move when

THEORY: Transitions

the time comes. I need to then discuss Mattias giving his tenancy up as the multidisciplinary group, and to an extent Mattias himself, are in agreement about medium-term residential care.

I admit that I am worried about his institutionalisation and the impact on his identity. It can take days to become institutionalised and months or years to change this mindset. I am worried about him taking responsibility for his own recovery. I will take this to supervision as this is huge.

Reflective questions

• How do I help other professionals see the person at the centre of complex issues?

• How do I balance the human rights issue of hearing the person's voice?

• How do I manage power imbalances within the multidisciplinary team around the person?

• If Mattias asks for his records from his time with Children's Services, to help his recovery, what would help or hinder from the way these are recorded?

• How can services around Mattias respond appropriately to support trauma recovery?

• How can I support others to handle Mattias' ambivalence about living and dying?

Further reading

Curran, L (2013) *101 Trauma-informed Interventions: Activities, Exercises and Assignments to Move the Client and Therapy Forward*. Eau Claire, WI: PESI Publishing and Media.

Foy, K (2020) *Acquired Brain Injury: A Guide for Families and Survivors*. Aberdeen: Ockham Publishing.

Juhila, K et al (2021) *Interprofessional Collaboration and Service User Participation: Analyzing Meetings in Social Welfare*. Bristol: Policy Press.

Thompson, N (2011) *Crisis Intervention: Theory into Practice*. Lyme Regis: Russell House.

Some thoughts to finish

Social work operates in the grey areas that the public hold us accountable for. I hope that these short stories have sparked some reflective conversations that will help you consider navigating this uncertainty, working with the competing needs, wishes and preferences of multiple people you meet in your own practice. I hope that by using the material you have developed some confidence to reconsider your own perspectives and to respectfully challenge the perspectives of others.

I hope that you go on to develop a sophisticated and flexible approach to using theory, critiquing and tailoring the application of this, and staying open to reassessing the changing needs of the people you serve. The toolkit we learn in training is only the start. Critical practice in social work practice is forever evolving. Experience and evidence-based practice changes the way we think and interact professionally and personally.

I hope you can achieve the confidence to readily 'show your workings out' – a skilled practitioner should be able to present and defend their decision making to anyone who has a right to question it, and to adapt communication so it is fully understood by all concerned. A proficient worker needs to be prepared to patiently revisit this again, never assuming the first time was enough, and accepting that their time is worthwhile to ensure practice is anti-oppressive.

However, we know that social work in the real world is usually difficult. One size never fits all. Maintaining constructive relationships while telling people things they don't want to hear, or working with competing or unspoken discourses for example, requires energy and resilience. It also needs a high level of self-awareness and we are not going to get it right every time.

Here are a few decision-making pitfalls to be aware of.

Anchoring bias	being overly reliant on the first piece of information
Clustering illusion	tendency to see patterns in random events
Blind spot bias	not noticing either cognitive or motivational bias in ourselves
Ostrich effect	ignoring dangerous or negative information
Resource bias	decisions actively influenced by availability of resources
Availability heuristic	overestimating the importance of available information
Confirmation bias	listening only to information which confirms our pre-conceptions
Recency bias (which is the basis of 'start again syndrome')	weighting latest information more heavily than previous evidence
Over-optimism	too confident in our decision and taking greater risks
Repetition bias	tendency to attach weight to the most repeated story
Similarity bias	favouring the information presented by people who are 'like us'
Conservatism bias	favouring prior evidence over recent information
Bandwagon bias (or group think)	safety in numbers makes people reluctant to appear to think differently from the group

Sunk-costs bias	following through on a course of action because we previously invested in it
Authority bias	basing decisions on the attributes and opinions of an authority figure and putting our personal opinion on hold

There are other psychological biases if you want to look them up – forewarned is forearmed! And to make matters worse, the more experienced we get, the more biased we tend to become. For example, if we have experienced something similar before, we are more likely to draw comparisons the next time. Although this means that social work experience brings valuable practice wisdom, it also means we may take shortcuts with our decision making.

To add to this, social workers of course undertake professional decision making alongside their own current experience and frame case narrative through their own world view. This discussion would not be complete without recognising the impact of a social worker's home life as a constant factor that will influence decision making, as well as the contextual experiences in the workplace. The emotional temperature of both are continually at play.

Therefore, organisations have a responsibility to ensure agency culture is conducive to robust decision making if they are serious about prioritising those who need a service. This includes attending to reasons that bring about ethical stress for workers and providing protected and valued opportunities for reflective supervision. Wider still, it is possible not to work at a persistent crisis level if the organisational focus is to keep a collective eye on decision making at the point of first concern, clearly ensuring that the right people are doing the right job and jointly not letting go of relationships until early risk has reduced and a robust network of support is in place. To enact this in real-world practice, the focus needs to move away from form-filling to analytical assessments which pursue outcomes that matter to people, making the system fit the person. Social workers, and the people they serve, need organisations to engage in discussions that recognise and address day-to-day systemic and contextual barriers to quality decision making.

Within teams we also need to carve essential time to support each other, to recognise the signs of fatigue in peers and come to a mutual agreement on how colleagues want to be assisted in their decision making. And there is no price that can be put on a supportive team who will help each other deconstruct the narrative when we are faced with dilemmas, to question and critique our presentation of the situation and call us out when we need it. Team support can guard against our own biases and blind spots. I hope you, and the people you serve, are lucky enough to find a team like this.

Index

safety, 64
satisfaction, 74
schema therapy, 54
secure base model, 20, 21, 62
self-determination, 57, 58, 64, 70
self-efficacy, 6, 9, 19, 48, 62, 71, 74, 80
self-regulation, 8, 20, 27, 35, 49, 50, 62, 70, 72, 83
sensitivity, 8, 14, 26, 53, 58, 64, 71, 77, 78, 86, 88
shame, 35, 41, 44, 62, 66, 77, 79, 81
shock, 26
similarity bias, 91
social bond theory, 49, 64, 66
social constructionism, 63, 70
social justice, 78
social learning theory, 17, 48, 63
social model, 44

socialisation, 17, 25
solution-focused brief therapy, 58, 72
stigma, 3, 6, 28, 35, 44, 47, 62, 79
Stockholm syndrome, 14
strengths-based practice, 6, 35, 79
stress, 26, 38, 42, 43
suicide intervention, 83
sunk-costs bias, 92

task-centred practice, 29, 45, 64
theory of mind, 17
tolerance, 54, 58, 62
transactional analysis, 6, 36, 42, 78
transitions, 6, 9, 42, 47, 78, 88
planned/unplanned, 22
transparency, 19, 20, 49, 53
trauma, 5, 17, 26, 27, 33, 38, 53, 55, 57, 71, 83, 84

trauma-informed, 85
trauma-sensitive, 4, 7, 25, 30, 37
traumatic dissociation, 26

unconditional positive regard, 49, 54
unmet need, 5, 14
early unmet need, 61
use of power, 34, 38
and authority, 7

validation, 38
victim theory, 25
vulnerability, 26, 38, 42, 43

window of tolerance, 35
world view, 69, 74, 83